ST. PETER'S BONES

ST. PETER'S BONES

How the Relics of the First Pope Were Lost and Found . . . and Then Lost and Found Again

Thomas J. Craughwell

IMAGE

NEW YORK

Library of Congress Cataloging-in-Publication Data is available upon
request.

ISBN 978-0-307-98509-5
eBook ISBN 978-0-307-98510-1

Book design by Jaclyn Reyes
Illustrations by Jaclyn Reyes
Cover design by Dan Rembert
Cover photography by Brideman Art Library

First Edition

147468846

To my friend and fellow relic wrangler,
Father Charles Jan Di Mascola

CONTENTS

ACKNOWLEDGMENTS

My sincere thanks to the generous, helpful, and patient staff of Image Books, particularly my editor, Amanda O'Connor, and my very skillful copy editor, Mary Anne Stewart—their thoughtful, meticulous editorial work improved this book immeasurably. My thanks to Jessie Bright, who designed the wonderful cover. And finally, a big "thank-you" to Gary Jansen—a great friend and my greatest champion at Image Books.

A Note on the Cult of Relics

For Catholics and non-Catholics alike, the typical response to relics of the saints tends to alternate between squeamishness and ghoulish fascination. In Europe especially, where it is not unusual to see crystal shrines that display a skull, a tibia, or a femur on altars or in cathedral treasuries, devout pilgrims as well as curious tourists often find themselves uncertain why the Catholic Church permits such a "medieval" custom to survive.

Of course, displaying and venerating sacred relics is not uniquely a Catholic custom. Christians of the Orthodox Church also preserve and revere relics of the saints. Sacred relics are not unknown among Muslims and Buddhists: Islam has the sword and mantle of the Prophet Muhammed, as well as strands of his beard, while Buddhism preserves bones and teeth of the Buddha.

Reverence for the remains of the saints is older than Christianity. In fact, it is rooted in Scripture, beginning with the Old

Testament. There is a story in 2 Kings 13:20–21 of an Israelite who was buried beside the body of the prophet Elisha. As his family and friends lowered the corpse into the grave, the dead man brushed against the bones of Elisha; instantly the dead man was restored to life. There are more examples in the New Testament. St. Mark the Evangelist tells of a woman who suffered from a hemorrhage for twelve years. As Jesus walked by her, she reached out and touched the hem of his robe—at once, she was healed (Mark 5:25–34). Finally, in the Acts of the Apostles, we learn that the first Christians asked St. Paul to touch pieces of cloth, which they carried to those who were seriously ill or possessed by evil spirits. As soon as the infirm came in contact with the cloths Paul had touched, "diseases left them and the evil spirits came out of them" (Acts 19:11–12).

During the first three centuries of the Church's history, Christians were the targets of sporadic but violent persecution. From the point of view of the Romans, Christians were criminals, enemies of the state who had no respect for Rome, the emperor, or the gods. As criminals they did not deserve honorable burial. It was not unusual for the Roman authorities to burn the bodies of Christian martyrs, then dump the ashes into the nearest river: that was the fate of the bodies of St. Blandina and the other martyrs of Lyon who were put to death in the city's arena in AD 177. Nonetheless, we know that from a very early date Christians made an effort to recover the bodies of the martyrs when possible. In this they were imitating Joseph of Arimathea, a secret disciple of Jesus, who found the courage to ask Pontius Pilate for permission to take Christ's body down from the cross and bury it.

A letter dating from about AD 156 is believed to be the oldest surviving account of Christians rescuing the relics of a martyr. During Emperor Marcus Aurelius's persecution of Christians, St. Polycarp, the elderly bishop of Smyrna, was condemned to be burned at the stake. After the fire had burned out and the ashes had cooled, the Christians of Smyrna searched among the cinders. "We took up his bones," the anonymous author of the letter wrote, "which are more valuable than precious stones and finer than refined gold, and laid them in a suitable place, where the Lord will permit us to gather ourselves together, as we are able, in gladness and joy, and to celebrate the birthday of his martyrdom."

In that one sentence is a summary of how Catholics and Orthodox honor the saints: by placing their remains in a suitable shrine, by treating them as something of inestimable value, and by offering Mass, or the Divine Liturgy, in memory of the saint on the day he or she was born into eternal life in heaven. That anniversary is generally called the saint's feast day.

A tradition that dates back to the beginning of the Church in Rome asserts that Christians managed to recover the bodies of St. Peter and St. Paul. Peter was buried in a cemetery on Vatican Hill, near the arena where he had been martyred. Paul's body was buried in a cemetery on the Via Ostiense, the road that ran from Rome to the port of Ostia. At some later date, a shrine was erected over Peter's grave, and Paul's bones were placed inside a stone sarcophagus. In AD 199, a Roman priest named Gaius wrote to a man named Proclus, a critic of the Roman Church, saying that if Proclus ever came to Rome, he, Gaius, could show him the tombs of Peter and Paul.

In the year AD 313, the history of Christianity had taken a dramatic turn. The new emperor, Constantine, published an edict that put an end to persecution of the Church, granted legal status to Christianity, and restored to Christians property that had been confiscated from them a decade earlier during Emperor Diocletian's empire-wide attempt to obliterate Christianity. Then Constantine went a step further: he favored the Christians above members of every other religion, he gave the popes the Lateran Palace as their residence, and he began an ambitious program of church construction in Rome and the Holy Land.

Some of Constantine's basilicas—including the churches of St. Peter on Vatican Hill, St. Paul on the Via Ostiense, and St. Lawrence—were erected over the tombs of the saints. Then, in AD 386, St. Ambrose, bishop of Milan, discovered the relics of St. Gervase and St. Protase, the first Christian martyrs of his city. Ambrose had the bones moved from their graves in a cemetery and into his cathedral, where the relics would rest in a place of honor. Installing the relics in the cathedral in the heart of town would be more convenient for the Christians of Milan who wished to pray at the resting place of these saints. Ambrose's decision marked the next stage in the development of the cult of relics—the movement (the formal term is "translation") of holy remains from a grave in a cemetery to a shrine in a church.

As in the case of the bones of Elisha and the cloths touched by St. Paul, relics often became the vehicle for miracles. In Book 22 of *City of God,* St. Augustine tells of the miraculous healings God wrought through contact with the relics of St. Stephen, the first Christian martyr.

Nonetheless, Church officials worried that some Christians might be led to believe that the saints had godlike power, or that the relics themselves worked like magic. St. Jerome assured a man named Riparius, "We do not worship, we do not adore [saints], for fear that we should bow down to the creature rather than to the Creator, but we venerate the relics of the martyrs in order the better to adore Him whose martyrs they are."

During the Middle Ages, pilgrims' enthusiasm for relics intensified. Churches, monasteries, convents, even members of royal families and the aristocracy vied with one another to assemble especially impressive relic collections. In more than a few cases, wishful thinking and gullibility entered the equation. The head of St. John the Baptist was particularly prized, and as a result, today, at least nine places, from Damascus to Bulgaria to Amiens, claim to possess the skull or a portion of the skull of the saint who baptized Jesus. (During the Middle Ages, there were probably many more reputed skulls of St. John.) The *Catholic Encyclopedia* published in 1911 found that more than thirty places claimed to possess one or more of the nails used to crucify Christ. Bodies of the Holy Innocents, the infant boys massacred by King Herod in his attempt to kill the Christ Child, were another favorite relic. Given the size of a little town like Bethlehem, it is not likely that there were more than a dozen baby boys aged two years or under, yet by 1500, the number of relics purported to be bodies of the Holy Innocents ran to the hundreds.

Such abuses made relics a target of the Protestant reformers—and not just in the polemical sense. In northern Germany, the Low Countries, England, Scotland, Switzerland, and other areas where Protestantism gained an upper hand, shrines were attacked by mobs, or dismantled by government officials, and the relics burned. In response, the Catholic bishops assembled at the Council of Trent (1545–1563) defined and defended the proper veneration of relics: "The holy bodies of holy martyrs and of others now living with Christ—which bodies were the living members of Christ and 'the temple of the Holy Ghost' (1 Corinthians 6:19) and which are by Him to be raised to eternal life and to be glorified are to be venerated by the faithful, for through these [bodies] many benefits are bestowed by God on men."

Guided by Trent's decree regarding relics, the Catholic Church continues to encourage the proper veneration of relics. Sealed within the main altar of every Catholic church are the relics of saints, thereby providing each parish with a direct link to the age of the martyrs, when bishops offered Mass in the catacombs, using the sarcophagus of a martyr as an altar. The exhumation and translation of the remains of a candidate for sainthood from the grave to a shrine is part of the Church's formal canonization process. It is common practice for priests to bless pilgrims or the sick with a relic, but always with the understanding that if a miraculous healing occurs, it is the power of God operating, according to his will, through the relic. It is understood that the relic possesses no power of its own.

In light of Catholics' abiding reverence for relics of the saints, the quest for St. Peter's bones is no mere Catholic Indiana Jones story. The desire to possess a physical link with a person we love or admire is deeply rooted in the human psyche. This desire expresses itself in many ways: wearing Grandma's pearls, visiting the Tomb of the Unknown Soldier, lining up to see the bloodstained gloves Mary Todd Lincoln wore to Ford's Theatre the night her husband was assassinated.

That same impulse prompted the archaeologists and anatomists and anthropologists who labored in the dark, dank atmosphere of the necropolis 120 feet beneath St. Peter's Basilica, and later in modern laboratories, where the bones and other remains were examined with all the care and precision the science of the 1950s and 1960s could provide. As scientists, they were called upon to be objective, to be dispassionate about what they were analyzing. Yet it was impossible to escape the bigger questions: Was St. Peter's tomb directly beneath the basilica's high altar? Were the apostle's bones inside that tomb? If so, these archaeologists and anatomists would have found a treasure "more valuable than precious stones and finer than refined gold."

Chapter 1

AN ELDERLY BUT POWERFUL MAN

In 1940, Pope Pius XII authorized a thorough reconstruction of the Vatican Grottoes, the undercroft of the Basilica of St. Peter, transforming it from a cramped burial chamber into a series of crypt chapels. To accomplish this, the floor of the Grottoes would be lowered by two-and-a-half feet. Everyone in the Vatican knew that there were Roman remains under the basilica, but no one had any idea what type—no one had seen them in sixteen hundred years. Then, in January 1941, workmen uncovered an elegant mausoleum that, based on inscriptions found in the tomb, had belonged to the Cetenni family. The archaeologists who were called in to examine the find declared that it was a discovery of genuine importance. On their recommendation, Pius XII gave permission for a full-scale excavation of the area beneath the Grottoes.

Pius's decision was daring. Other popes had expressed an interest in excavating beneath St. Peter's but had always held back out of reverent awe. Rome's Christians had buried the earliest popes and countless forgotten martyrs in the vicinity of St. Peter's tomb; it would be sacrilege to disturb the graves of so many saints. So Pius settled on a compromise. The archaeologists could excavate everywhere beneath the Grottoes with one exception: the area below the high altar and in the immediate surrounding area. The place where St. Peter was presumed to be buried was deemed off-limits.

To supervise and direct the project, the pope created a commission and named to it a group of expert scholars, as well as a team of *sampietrini*. Traditionally, the sampietrini are an elite corps of men trained in every trade and craft. These electricians, stonemasons, plasterers, and plumbers are responsible for the maintenance of St. Peter's Basilica, and they take this trust very seriously. The sampietrini are so defensive of the responsibilities placed upon them, that in most cases the job is passed down from father to son for generations.

The scholars included Professor Enrico Josi, a leading expert on the catacombs; Antonio Ferrua, S.J., considered the foremost scholar of epigraphy, the study of ancient Christian inscriptions; Engelbert Kirschbaum, S.J., a professor of Christian archaeology; and three architects, Bruno Maria Apollonj Ghetti, Gustavo Giovannoni, and Giuseppe Nicolosi. The manager of the project was Monsignor Ludwig Kaas, one of Pius XII's closest advisers, especially on Church-state affairs in Nazi Germany. Msgr. Kaas also was administrator of the Basilica of St. Peter.

This work crew assigned to lower the floor of the Grottoes had been laboring for about three weeks when on January 18, 1941, one of the men digging at a spot in the south aisle uncovered the top of a brick wall. The crew had been turning up sarcophagi almost from their first day on the job—that had been expected, as the Grottoes had been a burial place for sixteen hundred years. But finding evidence of a structure beneath St. Peter's had not been expected. The foreman sent for one of the Vatican archaeologists.

By carefully clearing away more soil, a portion of the wall was revealed: one side was plain, unadorned brick, and judging from its style, undoubtedly ancient; the other side of the wall had been plastered and painted a vivid shade of greenish blue. Gradually the sampietrini uncovered the top of a rectangular building, measuring twenty-two by twenty feet. Its roof was gone, deliberately removed, and the interior of the building had been filled with soil. But why? At this stage, the Vatican archaeologists could only speculate. In the meantime, they ordered the work crew to remove all the soil from the interior of the little building.

Once the building had been cleared and the soil brushed from the interior walls, the diggers and archaeologists found themselves standing in the middle of a beautifully decorated tomb. One fresco depicted swans bearing garlands in their beaks, another pictured birds amid roses and violets. The most elaborate scene portrayed Venus, the Roman goddess of love, supported by two tritons, or sea gods, as she rose above the waves. Carved into the walls were many niches, some of which held marble cremation urns, still in their original places, untouched since another work crew had packed the tomb with earth centuries earlier.

The floor was paved with a mosaic of black and white tiles.

In the center of the chamber stood an altar that revealed the identity of the owners of this tomb: Marcus Caetennius Antigonus and his wife, Tullia Secunda.

In addition to the urns, there were also terra-cotta sarcophagi sealed with marble slabs. These sarcophagi had been slipped into arched niches in the bottom half of the chamber's walls. One of these slabs marked the grave of a member of the Caetennius family (or Caetenni, as they would have been known in ancient Rome) who had been a Christian. The inscription reads:

ANIMA DULCIS GORGONIA
MIR(A)E I(N) SPECIE ET
CASTITATI EIVS AMELI(A)E
GORGONIAE QVI(A)E VIXIT
ANN(IS) XXVIII MENS(IBUS) II
D(IEBUS) XXVIII
DORMIT IN PACE CO(N)IVGI
DULCISSIME FECI

GORGONIA, SWEET SOUL.
TO THE WONDROUS BEAUTY AND CHASTITY OF
AEMILIA GORGONIA, WHO LIVED 28 YEARS, 2
MONTHS AND 28 DAYS.
SLEEP IN PEACE. I GAVE THIS BURIAL TO MY DARLING
WIFE.

Two Christian emblems were incised into the marble: two doves bearing olive branches, the symbol of peace, flanked by the phrase "Sleep in peace." To the left of the inscription is a woman drawing water from a well, an early Christian sign of eternal life. Vatican archaeologists estimated that the Caetenni had erected their family tomb sometime between AD 130 and 170, and that it had been in use for approximately two hundred years.

The archaeologists ordered the sampietrini to clear away the dirt that sealed the tomb door and to excavate outside the chamber. Soon they uncovered another treasure: an elaborately carved white marble sarcophagus. An inscription identified the deceased as Ostoria Chelidon, the daughter of a senator and the wife of a member of the emperor's staff. The lid was ajar, so the workmen lifted it. Inside they found the remains of Ostoria Chelidon. On her skull rested a hair net of golden threads. Shreds of purple cloth—a color reserved for members of the highest rank of Roman society—still clung to her bones. On her left wrist, a heavy bracelet of solid gold flashed in the dim light.

Either find, the Caetenni tomb or Ostoria Chelidon's sarcophagus, would crown the career of any archaeologist. Yet this was only the beginning of the excavation.

Directed by the Vatican archaeologists, the work crew began to scrape and prod the soil on either side of the Caetennius tomb, and very soon they found more mausoleums—each one stripped of its roof and its chamber filled with packed earth. They had stumbled upon a little village of the dead.

· · • · ·

On an autumn day in the year AD 64, Roman guards led an elderly prisoner into a long, oval-shaped arena. There, before the eyes of a jeering crowd, the condemned man—a Galilean fisherman-turned-preacher called Simon Peter—was to be crucified. Very likely he entered the arena carrying across his shoulders the crossbeam to which he would be nailed (the upright post of the cross would have been waiting for him on the sand). He would have been naked, or perhaps wearing a loincloth. The crowd would have been able to see on his bare back and broad shoulders the bleeding marks of the *flagellum*, a multitailed whip embedded with sharp bits of bone or metal to tear open the prisoner's flesh. A man would have walked before the prisoner carrying the *titulus*, a wooden board inscribed with his crime: "Incendiary." Once he was secured to the cross, the *titulus* would be posted above Peter's head.

A tradition that dates back to the apocryphal Acts of Peter (written in the second century) tells us that Peter told his executioners he was not worthy to die on a cross as his Master, Jesus Christ, had so the executioners humored him and crucified Peter upside down. That would not have surprised the crowd, who knew there was no fixed method of crucifixion. According to archaeologist Vassilios Tzaferis, Roman executioners had developed several methods of crucifixion. The victim's arms might be nailed to the crossbeam, or they might be tied. His ankles might be bound together and twisted sideways so that a single nail could be driven through both heel bones, or his legs might be pulled apart so that he straddled the upright beam with nails driven through each heel bone into the side of the cross. In such positions, the pressure on the chest muscles and the diaphragm make it difficult for the victim to breath. He must pull himself up by his arms or push his body up with his legs, but as the muscles tire under this exertion, the victim can no longer lift his body weight and dies of asphyxiation.

To prolong a victim's agony, Roman executioners invented the *suppedaneum*, or foot support; it supported the weight of the victim's body, enabling him to breathe, which meant he might survive for two or three days. The Jewish historian Josephus tells of a case when three crucified Jews took three days to die. More cruel was the *sedile*, a little wooden seat, on which the victim could perch if he was desperate enough—typically a *sedile* was pointed, so every time the victim tried to find relief, he impaled himself.

Upside down, Peter still would have suffered an excruciating death. Speaking to the BBC in 2008, Paul Ford, senior lecturer in exercise physiology at the University of East London, explained that the body is not designed to pump blood from the head up. If an individual is suspended upside down for a prolonged period, the blood begins to collect in the lungs and the brain. As the blood fills up the air sacs of the lungs, it becomes harder and harder to breathe, so Peter might have died of asphyxiation. Meanwhile, blood would also have been pooling in his brain, a condition that is also fatal.

· · • · ·

How did Peter the fisherman come to deserve such a painful and degrading death? It began with a disastrous fire.

On July 18, AD 64, just after nightfall, a fire broke out in some shops in a neighborhood between the Palatine and Caelian Hills, near where the Colosseum stands today. There was nothing unusual in that—in a city where most of the apartment dwellings and shops were constructed of wood, sparks from an exploding log in an oven or a few spilled coals from a brazier could set off a blaze. This fire was different, however. Fanned by summer breezes and fed by a seemingly endless supply of wooden structures, the fire raged across the city. It burned out of control for six days and seven nights.

The Roman historian Tacitus, who experienced and survived the fire, wrote, "Terrified, shrieking women, helpless old and young, people intent on their own safety, people unselfishly supporting invalids or waiting for them, fugitives and lingerers alike—all heightened the confusion. When people looked back, menacing flames sprang up before them or outflanked them. When they escaped to a neighboring quarter, the fire followed—even districts believed remote proved to be involved."

By the time the conflagration had burned itself out, ten of the fourteen districts of Rome had been destroyed. Emperor Nero was at Antium when the fire broke out, but as soon as news reached him he hurried back to the city. He directed crews of men to fight the conflagration, and once it had been extinguished he organized housing for the homeless. While the people of Rome were still dazed by the overwhelming loss of human life and property, Nero saw in the ashes of Rome an opportunity: he would build a new, grand, orderly city, with a rectangular grid of streets and well-built *insulae,* or apartment houses, for the people. He also planned a magnificent new palace for himself, the Domus Aurea, or Golden House, set amidst an immense park in the middle of town, adorned with artificial lakes, and dominated by a 120-foot-tall statue of himself.

The plans for a new palace had been a miscalculation on

Nero's part. The tens of thousands of homeless Romans resented the idea that Nero was designing a house of gold for himself while they were living in misery in jerry-built huts. Rumors began to circulate that Nero had started the fire to clear the way for his palace, that as the city burned he stood atop the Tower of Maecenas singing "The Sack of Troy," a work of his own composition. The accusations were false, but it was the type of tittle-tattle that could bring down an emperor.

To save his own skin, Nero proclaimed that he had discovered the guilty party: the Christians had burned Rome. The Christians were an obscure group, scarcely any Roman knew what they believed or how they worshipped, but there had been talk. It was said that Christians hated all non-Christians (in other words, everyone else in the Roman Empire), and that they practiced cannibalism (no doubt a misunderstanding of the Eucharist). As a mysterious, apparently nefarious unknown quantity, the Christians made ideal scapegoats.

No one knows how many Christians were rounded up— Tacitus says "an immense multitude." There is ancient tradition that among the victims were the apostles Peter and Paul. By burning Rome, the Christians had proved themselves to be enemies of the state, and so they forfeited the protections of Roman law and could be put to death in the most gruesome manner Nero and his executioners could devise. Tacitus writes, "Mockery of every sort was added to their deaths. Covered with the skins of beasts, they were torn by dogs and perished, or were nailed to crosses, or were doomed to the flames and burnt, to serve as a nightly illumination, when daylight had expired."

When it came to public executions, inventive cruelty was

commonplace in the ancient world, and it survived in some societies into the nineteenth and even twentieth centuries. In ancient Rome, slaves, foreigners, and criminals were considered subhuman. They did not possess the dignity accorded to citizens of Rome; therefore they deserved a degrading death. To this was added the humiliation of being executed as part of a series of public entertainments in an arena or amphitheater—this was standard procedure in ancient Rome. The historian Strabo tells us of Selouros, the leader of a rebel army on Sicily, who had been captured and taken to Rome for execution. He was set up on a platform designed to represent the Sicilian landmark Mount Etna. At a prearranged signal, the floor collapsed, and Selouros fell atop lightly built cages that contained wild beasts. The force of his fall did not kill him, but it did break the bars of the enclosures. Out sprang the beasts, which tore him to pieces.

About the year 110, during Emperor Trajan's persecution of the Church, St. Ignatius, bishop of Antioch, was arrested. He was considered such a catch that he was taken in chains from Antioch to Rome for execution. Along the way, Ignatius wrote farewell letters to several Christian communities. As he approached Italy, he wrote to the Christians of Rome, assuring them that he had no illusions about what he might suffer: "Let fire and the cross; let the crowds of wild beasts; let tearings, breakings, and dislocations of bones; let cutting off of members; let shatterings of the whole body; and let all the dreadful torments of the devil come upon me: only let me attain to Jesus Christ."

· • • ·

The site of St. Peter's martyrdom stood outside Rome proper, across the Tiber River, at a place called Ager Vaticanus, Vatican Hill, the area's most distinctive landmark. The arena, named the Circus of Gaius and Nero (Gaius is better known to us as Caligula), stood at the base of the hill in Vatican Valley. A short walk away, stretching along the banks of the Tiber, were gardens that belonged to the imperial family—they had been laid out a few decades earlier by Germanicus (his younger brother Claudius would become emperor) and Germanicus's wife, Agrippina, the granddaughter of Caesar Augustus.

Aside from the garden, the Vatican was not picturesque, nor was it heavily populated—the soil was poor, so there were few farms in the neighborhood. Worse still, the valley was infested with snakes and malaria-bearing mosquitoes. Nonetheless, crowds of Romans risked the snakes and the insects to see two of their favorite entertainments: chariot races and wild animal hunts in the arena.

Nero is best known as a would-be poet and musician, but he also fancied himself a charioteer. He competed often in the Circus of Gaius and Nero, and he always won (his fellow charioteers knew it was wise to let him win). At one end of the arena stood a beautiful obelisk imported from Egypt; it was known as the *spina*, and it marked the point on the racetrack where the chariots turned. Peter would have seen it when he was led out to execution. The obelisk still stands on the site of the arena, in the center of St. Peter's Square. Not only is it the only visible relic of the Circus of Gaius and Nero; the obelisk is also a direct link to the martyrdom of the first pope.

· • • ·

Typical of virtually all the outskirts and suburbs of Rome, there was a cemetery in the Vatican district. For sanitary reasons, burials inside the city were forbidden, so grieving families carried their dead outside the walls, laying them in the earth or, if they were well-off, entombing the deceased in a mausoleum. When Peter was dead, some Christians—we do not know who—claimed his body, or perhaps stole his body, and laid it to rest in a grave in the Vatican cemetery. The *Liber Pontificalis,* a chronicle of the reigns of the popes, records that about ninety years later, Pope St. Anicetus (r. ca. 152–160) "built and set in order a memorial-shrine to the blessed Peter, where the bishops [of Rome] might be buried." The shrine consisted of a niche flanked by two columns, covered over with a coat of plaster painted red. At the front of the shrine was a stone slab where the faithful left offerings, such as flowers, lamps, or perhaps a few coins. The shrine was known as the tropaion, Greek for "the trophy," or "victory monument," signifying St. Peter's victory over pain and death. Over the years, Christians scratched brief prayers into the plaster, imploring the intercession of St. Peter.

Many of the tombs in Roman cemeteries were built to resemble Roman houses—although on a smaller scale. An example of such a cluster of mausoleums survives at Isola Sacra, Sacred Island, at the mouth of the Tiber River, between Ostia and Porto, the two ancient harbors of Rome. Lined up side by side, the tombs have lintels, doorposts, and little windows—just like an ordinary Roman house. Some families added a terrace or erected a little fence in front of their tomb. Inside and out there were decorative elements such as terra-cotta bas reliefs, frescoes, and mosaics. The Isola Sacra cemetery was the burial place of the area's middle class—shopkeepers, traders, and craftsmen who had done well and could afford to build a family tomb. Before Constantine began construction of St. Peter's Basilica, the cemetery near the old arena would have looked like the one at Isola Sacra, but on a grander scale.

· • • ·

After the excavation of the Caetennius tomb, the next one the sampietrini uncovered was a disappointment. It was smaller and not as elaborately decorated. It had one memorable feature, however. There was a painting of the owner of the tomb, seated on a cushioned stool with a scroll open in his lap as he addressed a servant. This tomb stood to the right of the Caetennius tomb, and after it was cleared, the archaeologists decided to keep moving in that direction. It was a significant decision, because they were digging toward the area beneath the basilica's high altar, the region that had always been off-limits to excavators.

The next tomb, built sometime before 180, was especially exciting. The inscription over the door proclaimed that a wealthy former slave, or freedman, Gaius Valerius Herma, had built the mausoleum for himself, his wife, Flavia Olympias, their freedmen and freedwomen, and their descendants. Inside the large square chamber were many tall niches, each bearing near-life-size statues in sculptured stucco, or plaster, of members of the Valerii family and various gods. Among the most striking is the sculpture of a distinguished elderly man, probably Gaius Valerius's father or grandfather, and a distinctly creepy sculpture of Hypnos, the god of sleep, depicted as a man with the wings of a bat.

The household of the Valerii produced at least one Christian, Flavius Istatilius Olympius, who, according to the inscription on his tomb, died at age thirty-five. The inscription records, "He joked with everyone and never argued." Beside Flavius's name is inscribed the Greek monogram for Christ, the Chi-Ro ☧.

The fine stucco sculptures were a thrilling discovery, but the Valerii mausoleum held something even more exciting: on one of the tomb walls, someone had drawn, one above the other, the heads of two men. The Latin word VIBUS ("living") and the phoenix, a symbol of resurrection and immortality, were drawn on the forehead of the first man. The man below was depicted as elderly and bald, with a long beard. Whoever drew these images outlined them first with red lead and then did a finished drawing in black charcoal. This image maker was no artist, but the inscription that accompanied the drawings elevated them to real significance. The inscription read:

PETRVS ROGA XS HIS	*Peter, pray to Christ Jesus*
PRO SANC(TI)S	*For the holy*
HOM(INI)BVS	*Christian men*
CHRESTIANIS AD	*Buried near your body.*
CO(R)PVS TVVM SEP (VLTIS)	

The inscription is the key to the drawings—the first head represents Jesus Christ and the second is St. Peter. The inscription was also the first indication that St. Peter's grave was nearby, that the early Christians knew where it was, that they came to venerate the Prince of the Apostles there, and that they desired to be buried near him.

Tragically, since 1943, when the Valerii tomb was excavated, this crucial inscription has faded away. The soil preserved it for sixteen hundred years, but once the soil was cleared away and it was exposed to the damp atmosphere of the Vatican Necropolis, the inscription became ever more faint until it disappeared.

Encouraged by this find, the archaeologists directed the diggers to explore to the right and the left of the Valerii mausoleum, as well as across from it. Very quickly the sampietrini found evidence that there were tombs stretching in both directions, and that there were even more tombs opposite. In other words, this was a classic Roman necropolis, with houselike mausoleums running along both sides of a narrow street.

The archaeologists, Professor Enrico Josi, Father Antonio Ferrua, S.J., and Father Engelbert Kirschbaum, S.J., made regular reports of their progress to Monsignor Ludwig Kaas, the administrator of St. Peter's Basilica, but now it was time to request a private audience with Pope Pius XII. The finds in the necropolis were so significant, the evidence that the tomb of St. Peter was only yards away so strong, as to call for a change in longstanding Church policy: they asked for the pope's permission to excavate directly beneath the high altar of St. Peter's. Pius agreed, but under the condition that the public was never to learn of the excavation. There would be no announcement to the world until the dig was completed and the results thoroughly analyzed and compiled in a formal report. Josi, Ferrua, Kirschbaum, and Kaas swore to keep silent about their work.

Pius had one more requirement: the work must not interfere with the liturgical, devotional, and ceremonial cycle of the basilica. St. Peter's is and always has been a working church. Early each morning, dozens of priests process out of the sacristy to offer Mass at each of the dozens of side altars placed around the basilica. From time to time the church is the setting for a solemn ceremony of canonization, when the pope proclaims one or more candidates to be saints. Then there are the complex ceremonies of Holy Week, and the elaborate celebrations of Easter and Christmas. Pius would not permit any of this to be interrupted, even for so worthy an endeavor as locating the tomb and relics of St. Peter.

Once again the four men gave their word to the pope. Then they returned to the dig.

·· • ··

The man venerated as St. Peter was born in the village of Bethsaida, about a mile from the shores of the Sea of Galilee. His father's name was Jonah, sometimes given as John; his mother's name is unknown to us. The couple named their son Simon. He had a brother, Andrew. It is likely that Jonah was a fisherman, because his two sons became fishermen. As adults, Simon and Andrew formed a partnership with two brothers, James and John, the sons of Zebedee, who may have been neighbors from Bethsaida or perhaps lived in nearby Capernaum.

Holy Land archaeologist Father Jerome Murphy-O'Connor tells us that meat in first-century Galilee and Judea was expensive, except during religious festivals, when the meat of animals offered in sacrifice was sold at discount prices. Consequently, fish was an important source of protein. To preserve it, the fish caught in Galilee was either smoked or pickled. Whatever was not consumed locally was shipped to markets as far away as Rome.

The Simon-Andrew–James-John partnership thrived—the gospels suggest that the men owned their own boats and had a few employees. At some point, to be closer to his business, Simon moved to Capernaum. Tradition has identified the location of this house. According to three gospels, Christ stayed there and on one visit cured Peter's mother-in-law (Mark 1:29–31). A modern church has been built around the remains, which can be viewed beneath a glass floor.

But there is another house said to have belonged to Peter. Recent excavations at Bethsaida have uncovered a six-room house, inside of which archaeologists found a handful of tanta-lizing artifacts: a fishing hook, lead weights of the type attached to fishing nets, and a curved needle used to make and mend sails. Probably a fisherman and his family lived in the house, and it is difficult not to imagine that this house may have been the home of Simon Peter.

The gospels of Mark, Matthew, and Luke all tell the story of Christ healing Simon's mother-in-law. In his first letter to the Corinthians, St. Paul tells us that Peter's wife accompanied him on his missionary journeys: "Do we not have the right to be accompanied by a wife, as the other apostles and brethren of the Lord and Cephas?" (1 Corinthians 9:5). ("Cephas" is the Aramaic form of "Peter"; both names mean "rock.") Neither the gospels nor tradition tells us the name of Peter's wife. In Book III of his *Stromata*, or *Miscellenies*, St. Clement of Alexandria

(d. ca. 217) states that Peter had children, although he doesn't mention their names. In Book VII, Clement tells us that when Peter's wife was being led away to martyrdom, he followed her, comforting her, and urging her, "Remember thou the Lord!" Unfortunately, there is no way to ascertain if Clement had accurate information that long since has become lost or if he was repeating an old legend.

Yet another tradition claims that the martyr St. Petronilla (died first century?) was Peter's daughter. On the strength of that tradition, about the year 757 Pope Paul I (r. 757–767) moved the relics of Petronilla from the Catacomb of Domitilla on the Via Ardeatina, outside the walls of Rome, into the Old Basilica of St. Peter. The relics lie today in "new" St. Peter's under the Altar of St. Petronilla, which occupies a prominent location in the basilica, to the right of the Altar of the Chair. Nonetheless, there is no proof that Petronilla was Peter's daughter; it is more likely that she was one of the Christian members of the Flavii, a noble Roman family that in the first century produced three emperors—Vespasian, Titus, and Domitian—and three martyrs, Flavius Clemens, Domitilla, and perhaps Petronilla.

· • • ·

Simon and Andrew had been moved by the preaching of John the Baptist and become his disciples. John was a prophet who had left his home to live in the desert along the Jordan River. There he preached fiery sermons of the destruction that was about to fall upon the unrepentant, but those who begged forgiveness for their sins and accepted baptism from John's hand would be saved.

One day, John spotted Jesus at a distance and exclaimed, "Behold the Lamb of God!" Through the inspiration of the moment, Andrew left John to follow Jesus. Andrew's first encounter with Christ proved to be a powerful experience, because soon thereafter he told his brother Simon that he had found the Messiah, the people of Israel's long-expected savior. Simon went with his brother to meet this messiah, and as he approached, Jesus said to him, "So you are Simon the son of John? You shall be called Cephas" (John 1:42).

Ten more men would join Jesus as his apostles, including Peter and Andrew's business partners, James and John, and their neighbor, Philip. In time it became clear to the apostles that Peter, James, and John had become Jesus's most intimate friends, and that Peter was becoming preeminent among them. Whenever the gospels list the apostles, Peter's name always comes first. In some ways, Peter was an odd choice to be the Prince of the Apostles: he was rash, impulsive, and on at least one occasion violent (the night Jesus was arrested in the Garden of Gethsemane, Peter drew his sword and sliced off the ear of a servant named Malchus).

For all his failings, there is no doubt of Peter's love for Jesus and his—under most circumstances—unshakable loyalty. Peter had won Christ's favor, and also the favor of God the Father. When Jesus asked his apostles if they had any idea who he was, they suggested that he was John the Baptist, or Elijah, or one of the other great prophets of Israel back from the dead. Peter swept away such speculation with a bold assertion: "You are the Christ, the Son of the living God." Jesus replied, "Blessed are you, Simon Bar-Jonah! For flesh and blood has not revealed this to you, but my Father who is in heaven." Then Jesus declared, "And I tell you, you are Peter, and upon this rock I will build my church, and the powers of death shall not prevail against it. I will give you the keys of the kingdom of heaven, and whatever you bind on earth shall be bound in heaven, and whatever you loose on earth shall be loosed in heaven" (Matthew 16:13–19). The Catholic Church has understood that at that moment Jesus Christ established the papacy and gave to Peter and his successors spiritual authority over the Church and all its members.

Chapter 2

SEARCHING FOR THE NAME *PETER*

With Pope Pius's blessing, the archaeologists no longer had to scratch their way, inch by inch, through the buried necropolis. They could go directly to the most likely location of Peter's tomb—the area beneath the high altar. They began in the Grottoes, in the tiny chapel known as the Niche of the Pallia.

In a church rich in places of sacred significance, the Niche of the Pallia has special importance in the life of the Catholic Church and is bound to ceremonies and traditions that are centuries old. On the morning of January 21, the feast day of the adolescent Roman martyr St. Agnes (d. ca. 304), the pope travels to the Basilica of St. Agnes Outside the Walls, the church built over Agnes's tomb. There, he blesses two white lambs. After Mass, the lambs are given to the shepherd of the pope's flock at Castel Gandolfo, his summer residence outside Rome. The shepherd is especially attentive to these lambs. In May, he shears them and then sends the wool to a convent where the nuns will weave the wool into pallia. A pallium is a circular band of white wool with two appendages, one hanging from the front and another from the back. Black crosses are embroidered on it. The sisters make one pallium for each new archbishop the pope will consecrate that year. The night before the consecration ceremony, the pallia are taken to St. Peter's and placed in a silver chest in the Niche. There they remain overnight. The next day they are removed and carried to the pope, who will drape one pallium over the shoulders of each new archbishop.

·· • ··

For all the divine favor granted to Peter, when it came to the necessity of Christ's sufferings and death, he was as much in the dark as Judas. As the time of Christ's Passion drew near, Peter tried to cover his confusion by boasting that nothing could separate him from Jesus, that he was ready to endure prison and death with his master. Peter probably considered this a safe brag, since he never expected that Jesus would face prison and death. But Christ knew better; all four gospels record his sad revelation to Peter that before cockcrow, before dawn, Peter would deny that he ever knew Jesus of Nazareth.

On the night Jesus was arrested, all the apostles fled, but Peter and John followed at a distance. While Jesus was being arraigned before Caiaphas, the high priest of the Temple in Jerusalem, Peter remained in the courtyard, warming himself by a fire. Three people recognized him as a disciple of Jesus; out of fear, Peter denied that he had ever met Jesus. And all this he said with Jesus standing within earshot. After Peter's third and most virulent denial, Jesus turned and looked at his friend. At that moment, a cock crowed, and Peter, overcome with shame and sorrow, ran out of the courtyard, weeping.

On that first Easter Sunday, the Risen Christ appeared first to Mary Magdalen, then to the three women who had come to his tomb near Golgotha (where he had been crucified) to anoint his body, then to Peter. Days later, on the shores of the Sea of Galilee, Jesus asked Peter three times, "Do you love me?" In an agony of shame Peter tried to express as earnestly as he could how much he loved his Lord. With these three expressions of love, Peter expiated the three denials he had made outside Caiaphas's house. And Jesus rewarded him by confirming his authority over the faithful, instructing Peter to "feed my lambs . . . feed my sheep."

Peter was with the apostles, the Blessed Virgin Mary, and the other disciples when Jesus ascended back into heaven. They remained together for nine days in the upper room, the site of the Last Supper in Jerusalem, praying as they awaited the coming of the Holy Spirit, as Christ had promised. On the ninth day, which was also the Jewish feast of Pentecost, marking the fiftieth day after Passover and the harvest of the first fruits of the crops, the Holy Spirit descended on everyone in the upper room, filling them with zeal and courage and giving them the gift of tongues, the ability to speak languages they had not known before. Peter, as the leader appointed by Christ, left the house and preached the first Christian sermon to the throng that had gathered outside. Many men and women were converted that day, so that Pentecost has come to be regarded as the birthday of the Christian Church.

In the days after Pentecost, Peter and John preached together as a team. Soon the Jewish Sanhedrin, the Jerusalem high council that had tried Jesus, summoned them to explain themselves. They defended the new faith they taught, insisting that God had given them the authority to preach. To confirm that authority, God worked miracles through the apostles: the Acts of the Apostles record that as Peter walked through Jerusalem, the sick were healed when his shadow fell on them.

True to Christ's command to go and teach all nations, Peter went on a missionary journey to Joppa, Lydda, and Caesarea, where he raised a woman named Tabitha from the dead, healed a man named Aeneas of palsy, and baptized the first non-Jewish converts to the faith, a Roman centurion named Cornelius and his family.

About the year AD 43, Herod Agrippa I ordered Peter's arrest. The king had already executed the apostle James, the son of Alphaeus; he planned to execute Peter after Passover. As Peter sat in prison, chained to two guards, an angel appeared, broke his chains, and led him safely out of the prison. He went to the home of the mother of John Mark (who would write the Gospel of Mark) to announce to the Christians of Jerusalem that he was free. Then he went into hiding for a time somewhere unknown—the Acts of the Apostles do not tell us where.

A year or two later, the unexpected conversion of Saul, a notorious persecutor of Christians, made many Christians in Jerusalem suspicious. But the disciple Barnabas vouched for Saul's sincerity, so Peter, James, and John accepted him.

Afterward, both Saul (now known as Paul) and Peter went off on missionary journeys. Paul was inspired to preach in pagan lands, while Peter was drawn to preach to the Jews. This led to an unexpected conflict within the infant Church and between the two great apostles. Jewish converts kept the law of Moses, including the dietary restrictions and the rite of circumcising infant boys on the eighth day after birth. These Jewish converts insisted that all pagan converts to Christianity also must keep kosher and all the men and boys must be circumcised. Paul objected. These laws were a severe stumbling block to his mission to the Gentiles. Convincing non-Jews to give up pork and shellfish and to never mix meat with dairy would be difficult enough, but Paul could not imagine how he would persuade grown men that they must be circumcised. Furthermore, Paul argued that Christ had fulfilled the law of Moses, that it no longer applied to Christians, whether they had once been Jews or Gentiles.

In a vision, God had revealed to Peter that the kosher laws were abolished, but Peter kept the revelation to himself. When he dined with Gentiles, Peter ate whatever was placed before him; when he dined with Jews and Jewish converts, he kept kosher. To spare the feelings of Jewish Christians—many of whom felt strongly on this subject—Peter never even hinted that he believed they were extremists. But Paul learned that Peter was playing two sides against the middle and denounced him as a hypocrite. The quarrel caused a rift between Peter and Paul, and we do not know if the two apostles ever reconciled.

For some years, Peter established himself in Antioch in Syria, one of the most important cities in the eastern half of the Roman Empire. It was in Antioch that the followers of Jesus Christ were first called Christians. No one knows how long Peter remained in Antioch, or in what year he relocated to Rome, but an ancient tradition says that he arrived in the Eternal City on

January 18. At the conclusion of his first letter, Peter assured his readers that he was with the Church "at Babylon." In other early Christian literature, "Babylon" is code for Rome. Ironically, during the Protestant Revolt of the sixteenth century, Protestant writers and preachers would use the name "Babylon" for the Roman Catholic Church, to convey that she was now as corrupt and depraved as pagan Rome had been.

· • • ·

The archaeological team had been working for only a few months in 1940 when they began their quest to find the tomb of St. Peter. The search for St. Peter's tomb was risky, both because of the sanctity of the spot and also in light of the works of art that adorned the tiny chapel of the Niche of the Pallia. The team's first obstacles were two framed life-size mosaic portraits of St. Peter and St. Paul. Carefully, the sampietrini detached the huge framed icons from the wall and set them aside. This revealed a large brick wall, the upper part of which dated from the seventeenth century and the lower part from the late sixth or early seventh century. There was no way to see what was behind the wall except by removing a portion of it. One of the sampietrini took a hammer and chisel and chipped away at several bricks at the top center part of the wall. Once the bricks were removed, everyone could see a sheet of white marble with a band of dark red porphyry running up the middle. After some discussion, the team agreed that the brick wall must come down.

After several days of monotonous hammering and chipping, all the bricks were cleared away and the marble was fully revealed. It stood ten feet high, eight feet across, the porphyry band running directly down the center. No one wanted to smash the beautiful marble, so it was agreed that the porphyry band would be removed in the hope that the space between the two sheets would reveal what was behind the marble. And behind it they saw a wall of mortar. After more hammering, the sampietrini discovered a wall of plaster over brick. At the top of the marble wall they could see the base of a large altar. Msgr. Kaas and the archaeologists agreed it must be the altar Pope Callixtus II installed in 1123 and which today is enclosed in the altar consecrated by Pope Clement VIII in 1594 (Clement's altar is the one that stands today below the great baldacchino, or bronze canopy, beneath the soaring dome of St. Peter's).

More hammering and chipping opened onto dead air. The sampietrini made a hole large enough for Msgr. Kaas to get his head and shoulders inside. He cast the beam of his flashlight upward and saw yet another altar—the altar installed by Pope St. Gregory the Great in the sixth century, which Pope Callixtus had encased within his altar. It was interesting to see the altar-within-an-altar-within-an-altar arrangement, but in terms of reaching the tomb of the apostle, this had proved to be a dead end.

· · • · ·

In 312, two rivals for the imperial throne, Constantine and Maxentius, met at the Milvian Bridge on the outskirts of Rome. Few details of the battle have come down to us, except the most important one: as Constantine's men drove Maxentius's army toward the Tiber, Maxentius's horse lost its footing and threw him into the river. Perhaps Maxentius could not swim; perhaps his armor weighed him down. In any event, Maxentius drowned, and Constantine was proclaimed the victor and emperor.

No one in Rome knew it at the time, but the new emperor would change the history of the world. Constantine attributed his victory to the God of the Christians, the God his mother, Helena, worshipped. In thanksgiving for the divine favor, in 313 Constantine published the Edict of Milan, which granted freedom of worship to the Christians of the empire. This edict involved more than mere toleration—Constantine gave the once-persecuted faith preferential treatment and eventually became a Christian himself (he would be baptized on his deathbed). Almost immediately, he showered the Church with gifts, including turning over the Lateran Palace to the pope (it would be the official residence of the pontiffs for nearly one thousand years).

According to art historian Richard Krautheimer, in 312 the population of Rome stood at approximately 800,000, about one-third of whom were Christians or were sympathetic to the Christian faith. Since their religion was outlawed, Christians could not build formal places of worship; instead they gathered in houses or small mansions that they rented or purchased, or which were donated to the Church by members of the congregation. In 313, there were about twenty-five such house-churches in Rome, known by the name of the original owners, such as Cecilia, Chrysogonus, or Anastasia. Here Christians gathered for Mass, and also to baptize converts, to give religious instruction, and to dispense charity to the needy. The larger house-churches also had accommodations for the clergy.

Now that their religion was legal, Roman Christians began

to build a few churches. Krautheimer tells us they were plain, barn-like structures that blended into the shops, warehouses, and apartment blocks that stood beside or near these basic houses of worship. The interior probably contained minimal decoration, if any—not because Christians were iconoclasts (the frescoes in the catacombs tells us they had no objection to sacred images), but because most of the Christians of Rome belonged to the lower or middle classes, people who could not contribute much to embellish their churches. That was about to change.

Constantine expressed his enthusiasm for Christianity in real-world terms. He placed bishops on par with high-ranking imperial officials. Christian clergy and laymen joined his inner circle of advisers, including the Christian layman and Greek scholar Ossius of Cordoba and the pope, St. Sylvester (r. 314–335). He restored to the Church property that the government had confiscated during the persecution of Emperor Diocletian, and he gave to the Church estates and houses in Italy, Sicily, Sardinia, Greece, North Africa, Egypt, Syria, and Cilicia (in modern-day Turkey). By the end of Constantine's reign, the Church in the city of Rome enjoyed an annual income of 25,000 gold solidi, equal to about $175 million today.

Constantine found the stark, bare barn-churches intolerable; they did nothing to convey the power of Jesus Christ or the honor that Christ had bestowed upon Constantine when he made him emperor. The religion Constantine embraced and favored must be visible, its churches must rival if not surpass the temples of the pagan gods, the interiors must be a glimpse of the glory of heaven, exciting deeper devotion among Christians and drawing nonbelievers to the faith. Given Constantine's vision of what comprised a suitable place of worship, the shabby trophy over St. Peter's grave on Vatican Hill was entirely unacceptable.

Sometime around 325, Constantine planned the construction of a grand basilica that he would build over the humble tomb of St. Peter. It would require a tremendous amount of labor, not to mention engineering skill. The cemetery where Peter's tomb stood was in a ravine with a steep incline. Since the church would be built over the cemetery, the cemetery itself had to be stabilized. The solution proposed by the emperor's engineers was ingenious. First, the roofs of the mausoleums would be shaved off and the tomb chambers filled with earth to provide a solid base. Next, the incline of the ravine had to be leveled. Then, the foundations would be laid. It is said that at one point Constantine joined the army of excavators working at the site—in honor of the Twelve Apostles, he carried away twelve baskets of earth. While all this activity was in progress, the tomb of St. Peter had to be carefully preserved and kept visible so that the high altar of the basilica could be positioned directly over the remains of the Prince of the Apostles.

Rather than use pagan temples as a model, the basilica became the inspiration for Constantine's architects. In Roman society, a basilica was a long, rectangular public building where crowds gathered to watch as a magistrate held court. The emperor's architects designed St. Peter's with a wide central nave and two narrow aisles on each side. At the far end of the church was a semicircular area known as an apse; here the altar would stand, directly above the tomb of St. Peter. In Constantine's day, the high altar was the only altar in St. Peter's. The church was over 350 feet long, over 200 feet wide, and over 100 feet high. The interior could accommodate a congregation of between three thousand and four thousand.

Eleven large windows were cut into each of the side walls. The aisles were separated by eighty-eight ancient columns taken from pagan temples and other buildings. Outside, worshippers climbed twenty-five marble and porphyry steps to enter the basilica through any of five doors. Before reaching the church, however, they crossed a large outdoor atrium, or if they wished to get out of the sun or bad weather, they walked around the perimeter of the atrium beneath a covered colonnade.

The emperor's architects elevated the high altar, leaving an open chamber, called the *Confessio*, beneath so that pilgrims could see St. Peter's tomb. (The term *confessio*, or *confession*, refers to the confession of faith that Peter had made and that led to his martyrdom.) Especially privileged pilgrims would be permitted to enter the *Confessio* and venerate the tomb directly. It became customary for pilgrims to lower into the tomb chamber strips of cloth called *brandea*, touching them to St. Peter's sarcophagus, then carrying them home to be venerated as relics.

When the basilica was nearly complete, Constantine had St. Peter's remains transferred from its grave into a bronze sarcophagus. Above the sarcophagus he raised a golden cross that weighed 120 pounds. He plated the walls of the *Confessio* with gold and silver. Around the sarcophagus stood four tall bronze candelabra, and suspended over the shrine hung a golden oil lamp, constantly attended so that the flame would never be extinguished.

· • · •

The archaeologists agreed to examine the side walls of the chapel. Tapping gently, the sampietrini broke through; behind the wall was a narrow passageway about two feet wide. Father Kirschbaum squeezed sideways into it, and after going about ten feet, found himself inside a chamber about the size of a large closet. A portion of one of the chamber walls was covered with a slab of marble dating from the Middle Ages. Kirschbaum returned to the chapel and described what he saw. After a brief consultation among themselves, Kaas, Josi, Ferrua, and Kirschbaum authorized the sampietrini to remove the marble wall. Behind it they found yet another brick wall, and then another. In total, the sampietrini had to chip through four brick walls.

Once the walls had been cleared away—an arduous job given the cramped space and the narrow passageway out to the Grottoes—the archaeologists found a structure they could not immediately identify. The bottom was sheathed with white marble. The upper part was covered with red plaster. Perpendicular to the red wall was a four-foot-wide table-like slab of white limestone known as travertine, supported by a small marble column. The foundations of the structure appeared to go deep into the earth. Since they were unsure of what they were looking at, all four archaeologists agreed that the structure must not be tampered with; they would try the other side of the Pallia chapel and see if there was another passageway.

And there was another passageway, which led to another closet-size chamber, with another marble slab and four more brick walls to remove. This time, a plaster wall painted blue-white was revealed. The wall was covered with scratches. At closer examination, the scratches were found to be names and brief inscriptions. "There were names, more and more names," Father Kirschbaum recalled in his book *The Tombs of St. Peter & St. Paul*, "crowding on top of one another without any order and therefore almost illegible. They included large initial letters, carved with a rough tool in the blue-white plaster and others so delicate that they might have been scratched with a needle." Among the many names scratched into the plaster were Venerosa, Simplicius, and Leonia, and accompanying many of the names was the phrase "Vivatis in" followed by the Chi-Rho monogram, meaning "May you live in Christ." All the people commemorated upon the blue-white wall were deceased Christians, and for some reason, their families and friends chose this spot to memorialize them. The team did not know it yet, but the blue-white wall was adjacent to the red plaster wall, a detail whose significance would be understood later.

The team knew they were near the tomb of St. Peter, and they were almost certain these Christians had come to pray at the tomb of the first pope, yet nowhere in that tangle of scratch marks could they find the name of Peter. As authorities in Christian archaeology, they had seen many examples of such graffiti at the tombs of other martyrs, and almost without exception the pilgrims invoked Christ and the saint they had come to honor. The absence of St. Peter's name was unusual but not unique. Kirschbaum knew of at least one such example in Rome, specifically in the Catacomb of Priscilla, where a wall near the tomb of the martyr St. Crescentianus is covered with names and invocations scratched into the plaster, but the saint is never mentioned. "But," Father Kirschbaum added, "twenty paces from this cubiculum his name is mentioned explicitly in an inscription."

Nonetheless, the absence of St. Peter's name was disappointing—if his name had been among the graffiti, it might have been the first bit of evidence that they were getting close to the apostle's grave.

There was something else to raise the team's spirits: about two feet above the ground the plaster had fallen away, and there was a wide crack straight through the wall. Shining a flashlight through the opening, they saw an empty space lined with marble, like a burial vault. There was no entry without knocking down the wall of graffiti, which was unthinkable. Hoping there might be a way in on the other side of the structure, they returned to the Chapel of the Pallia and squeezed into the space where they had found the red wall and the travertine slab.

· • • ·

On August 23, 846, a Saracen fleet of seventy-three ships anchored near Ostia, the ancient port of Rome, and unloaded eleven thousand fighting men. They stormed into the city, then into the nearby town of Porto, and found both of them deserted. Thanks to a timely warning sent two weeks earlier by Count Adalbert, guardian of Corsica, the inhabitants of Ostia and Porto had packed their valuables and fled to Rome, where they prayed that the city's massive defensive walls would protect them from the raiders.

When word reached the city that the Saracens had landed, the Roman garrison sent mercenaries—Saxons, Frisians, and Franks—to drive them off. The mercenaries and the Saracens skirmished for the next two days, but there was no decisive battle. On the third day, as the mercenaries were seated on the grass enjoying their midday meal, the Saracens, unobserved, surrounded them. At a signal the Saracens attacked, and slaughtered almost every Saxon, Frisian, and Frank. The panicked survivors fled to Rome, but the Saracens did not pursue them. A force of eleven thousand was insufficient to capture Rome, and they had no siege equipment. But Rome was not the prize they were after. Through good intelligence the Saracens had learned that the basilicas of St. Peter and St. Paul stood outside the city essentially unprotected, guarded only by a congregation of Benedictine monks at St. Paul's and canons at St. Peter's. It is possible the Saracens found the two basilicas as deserted as Ostia and Porto, for the monks and canons may have moved into the city. However, the *Liber Pontificalis*, the chronicle of the reigns of the popes, which recounts the story of the Saracen raid, is silent on this detail.

The Saracens ransacked both basilicas, carrying off jewel-studded sacred vessels, gold and silver reliquaries, opulent vestments of silk and velvet and cloth of gold. Nothing of value escaped them. They even made their way into the shrine of St. Peter where they tore gold and silver plates from the shrine's marble walls.

On that terrible day in 846 St. Peter's tomb was not as accessible as it had been in the fourth century, when Constantine's basilica had been consecrated. According to Dale Kinney, professor of art history at Bryn Mawr College, at the end of the sixth century it was decided to raise the floor of the apse, or sanctuary. From that day, the tomb was obscured from the eyes of pilgrims, although a corridor was opened beneath the floor so that the pope, the canons, and privileged visitors could still have direct access to the apostle's shrine. It was by way of this corridor that the Saracens would have entered the shrine chamber.

In the nearly six hundred years that followed the Saracen sack of St. Peter's, Constantine's church filled up with altars, shrines, and tombs, all of which were enriched by some work of art in gold or silver, marble or alabaster or porphyry. The interior and the exterior of the basilica were decorated with mosaics, some dating back to the fifth century. Paintings, frescoes, and sculpture adorned even the columns of the church. As missionaries carried the Catholic faith all across Europe, St. Peter's Basilica became the goal of pilgrims from as far away as Scandinavia and Scotland. Macbeth—the real one, not the bloodstained monster of Shakespeare's play—made the pilgrimage to the tomb of St. Peter in 1050. As a king, he may have been escorted to the underground passageway that led to the shrine. If the basilica clergy did not regard him as important enough, then Macbeth, like thousands of other pilgrims, would have had to be satisfied with gazing at the altar that stood over the apostle's grave, because by 1050 the tomb was entirely out of sight.

But there were other relics to see. St. Peter's wooden chair, upon which he sat when he taught the first Christians of Rome, was preserved inside a reliquary in a side chapel. Every February 22, on the Feast of the Chair of St. Peter (which celebrates his spiritual authority, not the piece of furniture), the seat was taken from its shrine and exposed for the veneration of the faithful.

The Chapel of the Holy Face preserved the veil of St.

Veronica. According to a tradition that dated back at least to the second or third century, Veronica was a Jewish woman of Jerusalem who saw Christ carrying his cross through the streets. Moved by pity, she stepped out of the crowd and used her own veil to wipe the blood and sweat, the filth and spittle from the Lord's face. For her courage and compassion, she received a remarkable gift: when she returned to her house and looked at the soiled veil, she found the face of the suffering Jesus imprinted upon it. Legend says that Veronica journeyed to Rome, where she gave the veil to the pope. The relic had been passed down from pontiff to pontiff until it was enshrined at last inside St. Peter's. For centuries the veil was taken from its shrine only once a year, but during the Holy Year of 1300, Pope Boniface VIII permitted the relic to be exposed every week, thereby virtually guaranteeing that every pilgrim would have an opportunity to gaze upon the face of the Savior.

Yet another altar in St. Peter's held the bones of Saints Processus and Martinian, the Roman soldiers who had guarded Saints Peter and Paul in the Mamertine Prison. The apostles converted their guards, and when Nero learned of this, he had Processus and Martinian torn apart on the rack.

· • • ·

Above and below the travertine slab the archaeologists discovered behind the walls of the Pallia Niche were recesses cut into the red wall. In an upper recess was a window, such as the excavators had seen in the mausoleums in the necropolis below. That similarity between this odd-looking structure and the Roman tombs jogged everyone's memory, especially that of

Msgr. Kaas, who was a student of the ancient sources regarding the burial place of St. Peter. In 199, a Roman priest named Gaius squabbled with Proclus, a heretic who tried to assert the primacy of the churches of Asia Minor because the apostle St. Philip and his daughters were buried there. Gaius was not impressed. "I can show you the trophies [tropaion] of the apostles," he wrote. "If, in fact, you go out towards the Vatican or along Via Ostia, you will find the trophies of those who founded this Church." Gaius was arguing that the Church of Rome had preeminence among all the other Christian communities in the world because it had been founded by the apostles St. Peter and St. Paul, both of whom had shed their blood for the faith in Rome and were buried there.

The term Gaius had used was *tropaion*. "Victory monuments" is probably a better translation for tropaion than "trophies." Gaius had borrowed an athletic term, which was common among the early Christians when speaking of martyrs. Just as athletes persevere in their arduous training and then endure the challenge of competition to achieve the prize, so the martyrs strengthened their souls with prayer and penance so that they would have the courage and spiritual strength to lay down their lives for Christ and thus achieve the prize of eternal life.

Aside from Gaius's mention of the tropaion, no one knew how Peter had been buried. The apocryphal Acts of Peter, written ca. 150–200, tells of a Roman senator named Marcellus (he had been baptized by Peter) who took custody of the apostle's body: "And Marcellus, not asking leave of any, for it was not possible, when he saw that Peter had given up the ghost, took him down from the cross with his own hands and washed him in milk and wine: and cut fine seven minae of mastic, and of myrrh and aloes and Indian leaf other fifty, and perfumed his body and filled a coffin of marble of great price with Attic honey and laid it in his own tomb." Mastic was used to embalm a body, and one mina was the equivalent of sixty shekels, so Marcellus spared no expense in tending the body of St. Peter.

This account is almost certainly unreliable, but no other tradition, let alone facts, has come down to us about Peter's burial. As a poor man, the leader of a community of mostly poor Romans, his body was probably laid in a grave with some humble marker to identify the location. At this stage, Msgr. Kaas and his colleagues were not ready to identify the red wall and graffiti-covered blue-white wall as part of the tropaion of St. Peter, but perhaps it was an indication that St. Peter's grave was close at hand.

Chapter 3

THE CATACOMBS

Before moving on, the team of sampietrini wanted to inspect the marble-lined vault they had seen through the crack in the graffiti wall. Since there was no entry from the graffiti wall or the red wall, the archaeologists hoped to find another point of access, but that would require going behind the Niche of the Pallia.

To avoid the curiosity of visitors to the basilica, and to prevent distressing them by dismantling part of the Pallia shrine in plain sight, the team put off their investigation until after dark, when the basilica was closed. For two nights they met in the Niche of the Pallia chapel, and although a narrow opening behind the niche gave them another perspective on what might be the tropaion, there was no possibility of getting there without damaging the shrine, and that they would not do.

Together, the archaeologists and the sampietrini devised a solution: they would delve under the graffiti wall and enter the vault that way. One of the workmen chiseled away at the floor and wall below the crack until he could reach inside. Inspecting the marble box with his flashlight, he reported that the box was empty, but there was some debris lying on the bottom. He brushed everything into a pile and brought it out, laying it on a wooden board. The workman and the archaeologists found a coin from the Duchy of Aquitaine in France, minted sometime before 900. There were some small bits of lead and a handful of silver threads. And there were some tiny, hard objects, encrusted with earth. When these were washed, they were found to be splinters of human bones.

Everyone present wondered if the debris from the marble vault were clues. The vault once may have contained the body of an early pope or martyr, one of the many that tradition held were buried all around St. Peter's grave. Sometime in the Middle Ages, the relics might have been moved to a more accessible shrine, either in Old St. Peter's or in another church; this had been common practice for centuries (that would explain the presence of the French coin, which could have been dropped here by someone involved in the transfer of the relics). The team became even more determined to get into the area on the other side of the graffiti wall.

With a pick and shovel, a workman began digging up the soil. Eighteen inches down, the sampietrino uncovered a grave slab, with human bones beneath it. The archaeologists dated the slab as fourth century. The slab was lifted out of the hole, and the bones placed reverently in a wooden lead-lined box. The sampietrino with the pick went back to work. Four feet down, he found the base of the foundation of the graffiti wall, standing on yet another grave slab—and this one dated from the first century. It was a thrilling moment—they had reached the level of the necropolis where Peter had been buried.

· · • · ·

St. Peter's Basilica was a church steeped in sanctity, but by the fifteenth century it was falling down. The great seventy-seven-foot-long wooden beams that supported the roof had rot. Fissures had opened up in the walls as the building settled. Architects and engineers assured Pope Julius II that there was no repairing the ancient church. In 1505, when Julius announced that he would tear down Constantine's church and build a new one, many Catholics were scandalized: one would have to go to Jerusalem or Bethlehem to find a church more venerable than St. Peter's.

Concerns about the condition of St. Peter's did not originate with Julius II. In 1450 Pope Nicholas V had called in architect Leon Battista Alberti to inspect the old basilica. To the pope, the basilica appeared to be leaning, and Alberti confirmed Nicholas's suspicions—the south wall was six feet off plumb. After a detailed inspection of the structure, Alberti filed a report in which he stated, "I am convinced that very soon some slight shock or movement will cause the south wall to fall." If the south wall collapsed, the roof beams would pull down the north wall, and the entire basilica would crumble. In spite of Alberti's diagnosis, Nicholas hesitated; when he died four years later, no decision had been made regarding the future of St. Peter's.

Over the next fifty years, the basilica's physical condition became ever more precarious. It fell to Pope Julius II, a decisive, audacious man, to settle the fate of Old St. Peter's. He called in another architect to assess the church's condition. Donato Bramante examined St. Peter's and declared that the cost of repairing the church, including a major reconstruction, would be prohibitive, and probably only a temporary solution. He suggested tearing down Constantine's basilica and replacing it with a new church. Julius agreed, but between themselves, the pope and the architect decided that, to minimize the trauma to the faithful, the old church should be dismantled gradually as the new church rose around it. Consequently, over the next few decades, popes and pilgrims still had access to Old St. Peter's as construction progressed on New St. Peter's.

Shortly after Julius made his momentous decision, workmen began digging new foundations to support the massive piers of the new basilica. On April 18, 1506, Julius went in procession to the construction site with his cardinals, members of the papal household, and many visiting dignitaries. Attended by two cardinals and some stonemasons, the pope climbed a ladder down twenty-five feet into a trench to the spot where the base of what would become the massive pylon of St. Veronica, one of the four pylons that would support the church's great dome. Since early morning, workmen had been bailing water from the pit, but water still pooled in the muddy ground, and the atmosphere was dank and humid, smelling of earth and mold. Up above, the crowd pressed to the edge, which sent a shower of dirt down on the pope. Afraid that the weight of the crowd would cause the wall of the pit to collapse and bury him alive, Julius shouted an order that everyone was to move back.

The white marble foundation stone was waiting for him. He

blessed it. Then masons stepped forward and placed within a hollow carved into the stone a pottery jar containing bronze and gold medals commemorating Julius's pontificate. With his own hands, Pope Julius set the stone in place. After reciting a prayer to the crucified Christ and granting all present a solemn blessing, Julius, his cardinals, and the stonemasons climbed back to the surface.

The demolition of Old St. Peter's and the construction of New St. Peter's would take 161 years and span the reigns of twenty-two popes. Countless designs created and submitted by at least seven architects—including Raphael, Michelangelo, and Bernini—would be modified, rejected, and modified again until at last the basilica we know today, with its piazza and colonnade, was completed.

While the popes and their architects scrutinized blueprints and debated floor plans—Greek cross? Latin cross?—a demolition crew was set loose among the treasures of Old St. Peter's. The destruction began under Donato Bramante, the first architect of the new church. It was a public relations disaster. Bramante's men smashed altars, tore down walls with no regard for the frescoes or mosaics upon them, shattered columns—some of which had come from ancient Roman structures—and destroyed an untold number of priceless works of art. The Roman populace was furious and gave Bramante a nickname—*il Ruinante*, the Wrecker. As a result, very few works of art from Old St. Peter's have survived—just a few small fragments of mosaic, some sculpture, a few porphyry columns, and a handful of sacred images. One sculpture that did come through unscathed was Michelangelo's masterpiece, the *Pietà*. Vatican officials kept a close eye on the sculpture, moving it to one safe place after another as the demolition advanced. The *Pietà* is one of the very few treasures from Old St. Peter's that made the transition to the new basilica.

On November 15, 1608, the last Mass was said in Constantine's basilica, now little more than a fragment of a ruin. In the succeeding weeks, the last of the old church was pulled down.

· · • · ·

Early in the fourth century, about the time that Emperor Constantine put an end to anti-Christian persecution in the Roman Empire, Roman society experienced a shift in favor of above-ground burial. As a result, the catacombs, where Roman pagans, Christians, and Jews had buried their dead for the last two hundred years, were no longer active cemeteries; instead, the catacombs became destinations for Christian pilgrims who longed to pray at the tombs of the martyrs. To facilitate their visits, Pope St. Damasus (r. 366–384) improved some of the catacombs, adding staircases, digging shafts that let fresh air and natural light into the corridors and burial chambers, adorning the tombs of the most venerated martyrs, and composing approximately forty epitaphs that were mounted above the tombs of martyrs that Damasus held in special veneration. In spite of Damasus's improvements, the catacombs were inconvenient, especially for large groups of pilgrims who could not be accommodated comfortably in these cramped underground labyrinths. Over time, cave-ins and earthquakes made the catacombs unsafe to visit. To remedy the situation, popes in the eighth century authorized the removal of the relics of many of the martyrs from their graves in the catacombs to churches inside the walls of Rome. With the relics in the churches, there was no reason to visit the catacombs; soon most of these subterranean cities of the dead were forgotten.

·· • ·•

After more than a century of destruction of the old basilica and construction of the new, there was one thing the wrecking crews and the builders had not come upon—the tomb of St. Peter. The architects had kept track of where the high altar of the old church had stood so that a new high altar could be built on that precise spot. An unbroken tradition going back more than twelve hundred years assured everyone that directly below that altar stood the tomb of St. Peter, although no one had seen it in centuries. To confirm this tradition, the plans for New St. Peter's called for an open area in front of and below the high altar. It would be surrounded by a marble balustrade, or railing, with two bronze gates that opened onto two flights of marble stairs that led down to a small chapel known as the *Confessio*. Standing or kneeling at the balustrade, pilgrims could look down on the chapel, but very few would be permitted to descend. Over the years, in popular parlance the chapel came to be called "the tomb of St. Peter." It isn't. The best that can be said for this chapel is that it stands over the apostle's tomb. That is what the popes and architects hoped as they erected the new church. But they couldn't be certain.

The pope and the architects who supervised the construction of the new basilica hoped that as the construction crew built the Grottoes, or crypt, beneath the main floor of the basilica they would uncover St. Peter's tomb. In 1615, as the foundations for the *Confessio* were being dug, the workers found several bodies. One of the canons of St. Peter's, Francesco Maria Torrigio, published an account of these discoveries in 1618. One tomb, Torrigio said, held the remains of a man dressed in a chasuble, the long flowing vestment a priest wears when saying Mass. From his shoulders hung a pallium, the emblem of office for archbishops and the pope. The remains of other priests were also uncovered, and Torrigio was certain that the excavators had found the relics of Saints Linus, Cletus, and Evaristus, the second, third, and fifth popes. There had been a tradition dating back at least to the sixth century, to the first edition of the *Liber Pontificalis*, that Peter's successors had been buried near him. Writing of this discovery, Margherita Guarducci, a respected Italian archaeologist, classics scholars, and expert in ancient inscriptions, admitted the possibility that the bodies the work crew uncovered in 1615 might be of early popes, but she doubted that they could be identified as Saints Linus, Cletus, and Evaristus, because she doubted that the excavators had dug down to the level of St. Peter's original tomb.

In her 1960 book, *The Tomb of St. Peter*, Guarducci went on to describe an excavation in 1626, when workmen were laying the foundations for Bernini's monumental baldacchino, which would soar above the high altar. This dig went down much deeper, to the level of the cemetery where Peter had been buried. The excavators found a tomb, but not St. Peter's. It was a mausoleum, and inside the diggers found the remains of a pagan couple, Flavius Agricola and his wife. An inscription declared that the wife had been devoted to the Egyptian goddess Isis, while the husband had been devoted to pleasure. On his sarcophagus was a carving of Flavius, reclining upon a couch, clutching a wine cup in his hand. The discovery troubled Pope Urban VIII and his court. They had expected to find saints under the high altar, not pagan epicures. What if the tradition was wrong? What if St. Peter was not buried beneath the altar? Urban ordered that the work of laying the foundations should continue but forbade any further excavation of the area under the altar. As Guarducci put it, "It seemed better, all things considered, to respect the veil of prudent silence which the centuries had woven over St. Peter's tomb and to leave intact in faithful minds a consoling though unproven certitude."

It must have been a difficult decision for Urban, not least because for years a Maltese living in Rome, Antonio Bosio, had been hunting for long-forgotten catacombs and recording his findings. Of the forty or more catacombs outside the walls of Rome, only one had remained completely open since the days of the martyrs—the Catacomb of St. Sebastian on the Appian Way. A few others were open in part, in some cases with only a corridor or two accessible to pilgrims; these included the catacombs of St. Agnes, St. Valentine, and St. Cyriaca.

We can pinpoint the day interest in the catacombs was reawakened: May 31, 1578. That day, workers on the Via Salaria Nuova were digging up volcanic stone known as *pozzolana*. Suddenly they broke into a long-forgotten catacomb that ran beneath the vineyard of a farmer named Bartolomeo Sanchez. Exploration of the catacomb revealed sarcophagi, inscriptions, and paintings of scenes from the Old and New Testaments. The discovery caused a sensation in Rome. It also ramped up one of the greatest points of contention between Catholics and Protestants: the veneration of sacred images. Protestants liked to portray themselves as the true heirs of the ancient Christians, while dismissing Catholics as interlopers who introduced all manner of pagan corruptions into the Christian Church, among these, the veneration of images, which Protestants regarded as idolatry. The discovery of a catacomb filled with sacred art delighted Catholic apologists and discomfited their Protestant opponents.

Tragically, the catacomb vanished as swiftly as it appeared: the local pozzolana collectors had no interest in old tombs and old paintings; they just wanted the stone. They continued to work the site until the walls caved in, burying them alive. Only many years later would this catacomb be reopened and studied. The original explorers of this site concluded that it was a private cemetery, although they never learned the name of the ancient Roman family who owned it. Consequently, it is known as the Anonymous Cemetery.

Before the cave-in, three men, all amateurs, had begun studying the Anonymous Cemetery: a Spanish Dominican priest, Alfonso Chacon, or Ciacconio, and two Flemish laymen, Philip de Winghe and Jean l'Heureux. Later, these three would be the first to explore the catacombs of Priscilla, St. Valentine, Saints Peter and Marcellinus, and St. Callixtus (known at the time as the cemetery of Zephyrinus, after the pope who had opened it). None of these men were trained archaeologists (the science did not exist at the time), and their knowledge of early Christian society in Rome was not only limited, but often just plain wrong. Nonetheless, their work was a start.

While these three pioneers of catacomb archaeology were

studying the ancient burial grounds of the early Church, a Maltese boy named Antonio Bosio was making his way through the schools of Rome. His particular area of interest was early Christianity, specifically in Rome. At age eighteen he began spending his days in various archives across the city, studying the acts of the martyrs and the writings of the early Christian theologians and the first Christian historians. As he stumbled on little nuggets of information in his reading, he filed them away for future reference. Eventually, his notes on life and death in Rome during the first three centuries of the Church filled four massive tomes.

There were no maps that pinpointed the location of the catacombs, so Bosio wandered across the fields outside Rome, looking for a fragment of a staircase jutting out of the ground, or an overgrown entrance to a tunnel, or a narrow pit that might be one of the shafts Pope Damasus had installed twelve hundred years earlier. In this way he found approximately thirty burial places, including a Jewish catacomb. Although he never had the money to fund a full excavation of any of the catacombs he discovered, Bosio did make a preliminary exploration of the catacombs. He became known as "the Columbus of underground Rome."

Bosio's primary interest in the catacombs was religious. He saw the catacombs as definitive proof that the early Christians were Catholics, not proto-Protestants, as the Lutherans, Calvinists, Anglicans, and other Protestant denominations insisted. The inscriptions and the paintings in the catacombs showed the early Christians gathering around their bishop, priests, and deacons to celebrate Mass and the sacraments. They also revealed that the early Christians venerated the saints, their relics, and sacred images. In the religious debate that raged in Bosio's lifetime, he believed that the catacombs were the Catholic Church's trump card.

Bosio's discoveries did not set off a wave of scholarly interest in the catacombs, although they did attract grave robbers, who pilfered any artifact that might have value on the antiquities market. It was not until the nineteenth century that the catacombs at last became an object of intense scientific study.

• • • •

The interest of Giovanni Battista de Rossi (1822–1894) in the catacombs began at age eleven, when his father gave him a copy of Bosio's book, *Roma Sotteranea* (*Subterranean Rome*). De Rossi became a student of Giuseppe Marchi, S.J., a Jesuit priest and expert in early Christian monuments. In his early twenties, De Rossi accepted a post in the Vatican Library, where he took special interest in cataloguing early Christian inscriptions. With Father Marchi as his guide, De Rossi began visiting the catacombs. Soon, like Bosio, he was tramping around the countryside, looking for signs of long-forgotten subterranean cemeteries. He found about ten.

One day in 1849, De Rossi was examining a vineyard on the Appian Way. In a cellar he found a broken marble tablet that bore an incomplete inscription: NELIUS . MARTYR. From a seventh-century guide to the catacombs, De Rossi knew that after his martyrdom in 253, Pope St. Cornelius had been buried nearby. De Rossi appealed to Pope Pius IX to purchase this vineyard as well as the vineyard adjoining it so that he could begin an excavation. De Rossi dug for three years before he found the other half of the grave slab: it bore the letters COR and, beneath the pope's name, EP, an abbreviation of episcopus, meaning "bishop."

As the excavations continued, De Rossi found the chamber where St. Cornelius had been buried originally, the Crypt of Lucina. Lucina was a Christian and a member of a wealthy noble Roman family. Like many other well-to-do Christians of the time, she made room for the bodies of martyrs in her family tomb. By doing so, Lucina was not merely practicing the virtue of charity; she was also securing for herself and her family the prayers of St. Cornelius. Since his body was buried among Lucina's family, the martyred pope could be relied upon to intercede for her and all her relatives.

The Crypt of Lucina was in the Catacomb of St. Callixtus, which would prove to be one of the most fascinating of all the ancient Christian cemeteries. As De Rossi continued his explorations, he found the original tombs of St. Cecilia, a wealthy woman martyred in the third century, and St. Tarsisius, an adolescent boy who gave his life rather than permit a pagan mob to desecrate the Blessed Sacrament. Perhaps most wonderful of all was a chapel where nine popes of the third and fourth centuries had been buried.

Naturally, De Rossi reported his finds to Pope Pius IX, and on May 11, 1854, the pope, with a small entourage, arrived at the catacomb. De Rossi led his visitors to the crypt of the popes. In his memoirs De Rossi records the pope as saying, "So these, then, really are the tombstones of the first successors of Peter, the tombs of my predecessors who now repose here?"

De Rossi assured him that was correct; then he handed to Pius several of the tomb slabs of the martyred popes. The pope's eyes filled with tears. He knelt and prayed silently for a while.

In many cases, the original tombs of the martyrs that De Rossi discovered were empty, the relics having been moved centuries earlier to churches in the city. The bones of St. Cecilia, for example, lay in the beautiful basilica built over her mansion in the Trastevere district of Rome, and the bones of St. Tarsisius were placed in the Church of San Silvestro in Capite (exactly where the boy-martyr's relics were entombed is unknown—over time the location has been forgotten). But there were many graves that remained intact, with the bones of martyrs preserved inside. Many of these were new to the Church—their names did not appear in the Roman Martyrology, the ancient list of martyrs from the first centuries of the Church.

When such tombs were found, the bones, the inscription on the tomb slab, and any objects found within the grave were examined by historians and physicians for evidence that the deceased had been a Christian and died a violent death. For example, in 1853, during excavations at the Cemetery of Pretextatus on the Appian Way, the work crew found an intact tomb. The slab bore the inscription ANIMAE INNOCENTI ADQUE PUDICAE VIBIANAE IN PACE D. PR. K. ST, TO THE SOUL OF THE INNOCENT AND PURE VIBIANA, "laid away the day before the kalends of September" (August 31). The slab bore a carving of a laurel wreath, a Christian symbol for a martyr. Inside the tomb was the skeleton of a young woman and a small glass vial—it was a custom among the early Roman Christians to collect some of a martyr's blood (if possible) and place it in the tomb. After examining the bones, physicians concluded that Vibiana had died in a violent manner. The report regarding Vibiana eventually reached Pope Pius IX, who exercised his authority to declare Vibiana a saint.

By chance, a few weeks later, Thaddeus Amat, the new bishop of Monterey, California, arrived in Rome for a private audience with the pope. In Rome, the United States was regarded as mission territory, no different than the Congo or China. And in fact, in many places American bishops looked to Catholic Europe for priests to staff their parishes and nuns to staff their schools and hospitals, and relied upon the generosity of European Catholics to furnish their churches with altars, vestments, relics, sacred vessels—everything necessary for parish life. During his audience with Bishop Amat, Pope Pius had an inspiration: he presented the relics of St. Vibiana to the diocese of Monterey, to be enshrined in the cathedral.

Bishop Amat's diocese was not the only one in America to receive the relics of an early Roman martyr. Old St. Mary's Church in Cincinnati, Ohio, was given the relics of St. Martura. The Redemptorist fathers who staffed the Church of the Most Holy Redeemer in New York City were given the relics of St. Datian. The relics of a child-martyr, eight-year-old St. Cessianus, were Pope Pius's gift to the bishop of Dubuque, Iowa; the relics lie beneath the main altar of the Cathedral of St. Raphael. The skeletons of two martyrs, St. Bonosa and St. Magnus, were enshrined in the Church of St. Martin of Tours in Louisville, Kentucky. The chapel of the Sisters of the Precious Blood in Maria Stein, Ohio, preserves the relics of Saints Concordia, Victoria, Innocent, Cruser, and Rogatus. And the skeleton of St. Demetrius can be found in Pittsburgh's St. Anthony's Chapel, home to the largest collection of sacred relics in the United States. Unfortunately, nothing was known about these martyrs other than their names and the fact of their martyrdom. In the mind of Pius IX, however, that was enough to venerate them as saints.

From this bumper crop of newfound saints, one in particular became a phenomenon: St. Philomena. Her intact tomb was discovered in the Catacomb of Priscilla in 1802. An inscription painted on the three tiles that sealed the tomb read: PAX TECUM FILUMENA, "Peace be with you, Philomena." Painted on the tiles were an anchor, a palm frond, and three arrows. Inside were the remains of an adolescent girl, between thirteen and fifteen years of age. To keep the relics safe, the bones and the three inscribed tiles were removed from the catacomb and placed in a Church storage facility.

In 1805, a priest, Francesco de Lucia, requested the relics of a martyr for a new altar he was installing in his church in Mugnano del Cardinale, a town near Naples. He was given the relics of St. Philomena. Although nothing was known about this young martyr except the fact of her death (the painting of arrows on her grave slab suggested that she may have been shot to death by archers), an intense devotion to Philomena sprang up in Mugnano del Cardinale and soon spread throughout the Catholic world. Prominent Catholics, including St. John Vianney, St. John Neumann, St. Damien de Veuster, St. Peter Julian Eymard, St. Madeleine Sophie Barat, St. Frances Xavier Cabrini, Blessed Bartolo Longo, Blessed Anna Maria Taigi, and Venerable Pauline-Marie Jaricot, all cherished the saint and recommended her as a powerful intercessor in heaven. Pope Gregory XVI approved devotion to St. Philomena; Pius IX, Leo XII, and

Pius X all were devoted to St. Philomena. Churches and schools were dedicated to her from Ireland to India, from Canada to Chile. She was taken as the patron saint of infants, children, and teenagers; priests, prisoners, and test takers; people in financial difficulty and couples struggling with infertility. Of all the saints found in the catacombs in the nineteenth century, none became the focus of devotion like St. Philomena.

Yet, throughout the nineteenth century, as amateur archaeologists were tunneling all around Rome, hoping to find relics of long-forgotten martyrs and artifacts of early Christians, one place remained unexplored: no one was digging beneath the high altar of St. Peter's Basilica in search of the bones of the first pope.

·· • • ··

When the sampietrini reached the base of the blue graffiti wall, which everyone involved in the excavation hoped would lead them to the tomb of St. Peter, the team altered its plans. The archaeologists called for the excavator to come out of the pit, while a man skilled with hammer and chisel was sent in. Gently, he chipped away at the mortar, passing brick after brick up to the top. The graffiti wall proved to be two feet thick, and it took almost all day for the chisel man to break through to the other side and make an opening large enough for a person to pass through.

No one had dared to say that this might be the tomb of St. Peter, but the thought was in everyone's mind. Father Kirschbaum entered first, or rather was shoved in by a couple of sampietrini until his head and shoulders had squeezed through the opening. In a state of nervous excitement, he threw the beam of his flashlight from one part of the grave to another. Once he had calmed himself, he began a thorough examination of the burial chamber.

He examined the walls of the grave: they were irregular, not perfectly square, and each side was not quite three feet long—about half the size of a typical Roman burial chamber. The walls were a mix of packed earth and ancient brickwork.

He shone the flashlight up to the ceiling: it was a marble slab bearing a lengthy inscription that he could not decipher beyond the name, P. Aelius Isidorus. A small, square hole had been neatly chiseled through the slab. It was clear to Kirschbaum that someone at some point had expropriated Aelius Isidorus's tombstone, flipped it over, and used it to seal another grave. Shining his light through the square hole, he could see a shaft lined with green porphyry. He also noticed that the ceiling slab was ajar and that the ledge or lip that supported it was badly damaged, as if it had been battered with a hammer or some other heavy tool. And there was a small marble column that was out of kilter.

Suddenly the beam of Kirschbaum's flashlight caught the glint of golden metal. He reached up and felt a little metallic plate embedded in the wall. Kirschbaum pulled. "It was not easy to prise loose," he wrote, "and the seeker for gold was rewarded with a shower of mortar fragments in his face." Once he had brushed the mess from his eyes, Father Kirschbaum recognized the plate as an ex-voto, a devotional object brought to a saint's shrine in thanksgiving for prayers answered. The plate bore the image of a cross and two eyes, an indication that some Christian with an eye affliction had slipped this into Peter's tomb to thank the saint for his intercession, which led to a cure. In many Catholic countries it was still the custom (and it remains so today) to leave such an ex-voto at a shrine; Kirschbaum estimated this ex-voto dated to the sixth or seventh century. And it was made of gold. He passed it out to his colleagues.

Next he examined the floor of the grave—it was littered with coins. Age had turned them black, and in his current less-than-ideal circumstances he could not decipher any of the inscriptions, but by touch he knew that some of them were Roman, bearing the images of long-dead emperors.

Kirschbaum was working methodically now, casting the light slowly over each wall, watchful for more artifacts. That is when he noticed a small opening shaped like an inverted V at the base of the red wall. On impulse, he stuck his hand inside—the hole was filled with dirt. He began to dig, and as he did so his fingers felt something hard. He hesitated for a moment, then went back to digging. It took no time at all to clear the object from the soil, and when he pulled it out he found that he was holding a human bone, about five inches long. A feeling of dread and awe came over him: he was an archaeologist, but he was also a Roman Catholic priest, and he was holding in his hand a bone that might belong to St. Peter, the first pope. Shining his flashlight into the opening, he saw inside many bones piled at random. He replaced the bone he'd uncovered, squirmed out of the hole, and climbed out of the pit. As calmly as he could, Kirschbaum explained to his colleagues and the sampietrini what he had found. Immediately, one of the archaeologists ran to tell Pope Pius XII.

When he described this moment in his book, Father Kirsch-baum dropped the first-person narrative and switched to the formal, distant third person: "These bones are not remains from different graves gathered together, but in the judgment of experts, they form the skeleton of a single man, and more precisely of an elderly but powerful man."

Minutes later the pope, dressed in his immaculate white cassock, arrived at the dig. Father Kirschbaum explained what he had found, and after a brief discussion with other members of the team, Pius authorized them to bring out the bones. The sampietrini brought the pope a chair, and at his feet they arranged a series of lead-lined wooden boxes to receive the remains.

Taking a trowel and a brush, Kirschbaum squeezed back into the grave chamber. It took several hours for him to pass up the many bones he found. Some were large and relatively intact; others were fragile from decay; still others were tiny and may not have been human remains at all, but Kirschbaum did not want to risk leaving anything behind. Ultimately, he collected about 250 bones and fragments, which were reverently laid inside three boxes.

All of them knew, probably the sampietrini included, that for a thousand years the Church had believed that the balda-cchino over the high altar in the Basilica of St. John Lantern—Rome's cathedral—held two reliquaries, one said to contain the skull of St. Paul, the other the skull of St. Peter. The reliquaries had been opened in 1804, and cranial bones were found inside. Among the bones recovered by Father Kirschbaum, there was no skull. Although all the men at the dig restrained themselves from suggesting that they may have just recovered the bones of

St. Peter, the absence of a skull must have made it difficult to keep silent: the presence of skull bones in the Lateran and the absence of a skull in this grave beneath St. Peter's fit the oral tradition perfectly.

Pius thanked the archaeologists and the sampietrini. Then he ordered the boxes locked and had them taken to his private apartments in the Apostolic Palace.

Chapter 4

PAPAL PRUDENCE

While the archaeological team and the sampietrini were excavating and studying beneath St. Peter's high altar, in the outside world Europe, Asia, North Africa, and part of Australia were being torn apart by World War II. In July 1943, Allied troops landed in Italy; in September of the same year, Nazi forces occupied Rome. In October, the Nazis began a roundup of Jews in the city. Of the approximately eight thousand Jews in Rome at the time, the Nazis seized fewer than two thousand. According to Israeli diplomat, historian, and theologian Pinchas Lapide, Pope Pius had thousands of Jews concealed in monasteries, convents, and churches across Rome, with as many as three thousand sheltering in Castel Gandolfo, the pope's summer residence. On June 5, 1944, the Allies liberated Rome, and on April 25, 1945, all of Italy was freed from Nazi occupation.

By the end of the eventful year 1945, the archaeological team had completed their work in the necropolis. Nineteen mausoleums had been emptied of soil, as had the narrow street along which these family tombs had been built. The interiors and exteriors had been swept clean of dirt, their murals, mosaics, sculpture, and sarcophagi carefully examined and photographed; the many more simple graves that the archaeologists had found had all been opened and their contents recorded; the layout of the street, the positions of the tombs and graves, had been drawn meticulously to scale. Now the archaeologists were ready to begin writing their report.

·· • ··

No crucifix hung over the three boxes of bones from St. Peter's tomb. No candles burned before them. No vases of flowers decorated the table on which they stood. Pope Pius XII did not make a home altar for the bones, because he was maintaining a strict neutrality about their possible identity.

Shortly after the boxes had been placed in his apartment, he called in several medical men, including his personal physician, Riccardo Galeazzi-Lisi, to inspect the bones. The doctors concluded that the bones were of a man about sixty-five or seventy years old at the time of his death. In life he had been brawny, undoubtedly from a lifetime of physical labor. This agreed with the traditional idea of St. Peter, a man who had grown strong by hauling up heavy nets filled with fish. No one knew Peter's age precisely, but typically he was thought to have been about seventy when he was martyred. Nonetheless, Pope Pius was not convinced that the remains of St. Peter had been found.

Meanwhile, the archaeologists who had directed the excavations of the Vatican Necropolis were writing their report on the dig. The professional archaeological community demanded the highest standards regarding measurements, description of the sites uncovered, the location of artifacts, the position of the various tombs and graves discovered. Such meticulous attention to detail, supplemented by photographs and drawings, would take an enormous amount of time. To give the team the time they needed, Pope Pius chose an auspicious occasion to release the findings: 1950. Every fifty years since 1300 (with a few exceptions) the Catholic Church had observed a Holy Year marking the anniversary of the birth of Jesus Christ. During a Holy Year, pilgrims flocked to Rome to pray in the basilicas of St. Peter, St. Paul Outside the Walls, St. Mary Major, and St. John Lateran. By praying in all four of these churches, the Catholic faithful were granted a plenary indulgence, which is a full remission, or wiping away, of any time they might have been obliged to spend in Purgatory as atonement for their sins. The pope's announcement that the grave of St. Peter had been found would make the 1950 Holy Year especially memorable.

On Christmas Eve, December 24, 1950, Pope Pius XII broadcast a radio address to the world. "Has Peter's tomb really been found?" the pope asked. "To this question the answer is beyond all doubt yes. The tomb of the Prince of the Apostles has been found. Such is the final conclusion after all the labor and study of these years. A second question, subordinate to the first, refers to the relics of St. Peter. Have they been found? At the side of the tomb remains of human bones have been discovered. However, it is impossible to prove with certainty that they belong to the body of the apostle. This still leaves intact the historical reality of the tomb itself."

Pius's prudence in the matter of the bones was well founded. Nothing had been discovered in the tomb to prove conclusively that the bones were those of St. Peter. Furthermore, the location of the bones was troubling. If these were the remains of St. Peter, why would such sacred and significant relics be stuffed in a hole in a wall? There was an old story that when the Saracens sacked St. Peter's in 846 they broke open St. Peter's shrine and scattered the bones across the basilica's floor. If that were true, once the Saracen raiders were gone, wouldn't the pope have had the relics collected and placed reverently in a shrine, or at least a chest of some kind? For greater security, the reliquary could have been sealed inside an altar. The location of the bones and the condition in which Father Kirschbaum found them was troubling, because it was inconsistent with the manner in which Catholics have always treated relics of the saints.

As time went on and still Pius issued no definitive statement regarding the identity of the bones, many people who had been involved in the excavation, or knew of the existence of the bones after the 1950 radio broadcast, began to incline toward the opinion ("hunch" might be a better word) that the bones were those of St. Peter and that the pope was being unduly cautious. Father Kirschbaum went so far as to publish his opinion: "Who, we may well ask, is this old man in St. Peter's grave? In view of the fact that the head of the apostle has for many centuries been preserved and venerated in the Lateran church, the conclusion that these are the bones of the apostle himself is well nigh irresistible."

Even if Father Kirschbaum's statement is an example of wishful thinking, it is understandable. He and his colleagues had found Peter's grave exactly where ancient tradition said it would be—directly below the basilica's high altar. Inside the grave were the bones of an elderly man of powerful build. Granted, the location of the bones was perplexing, but Kirschbaum, among others, was willing to overlook it.

· • · · ·

Nonetheless, the bones remained in limbo until 1956, when Pius XII instructed Monsignor Primo Principi, the new administrator of St. Peter's Basilica (Msgr. Ludwig Kaas had died in 1952), to bring in the finest anthropologists to examine the bones. Msgr. Principi invited one of the most respected anatomists and anthropologists in Europe, Venerando Correnti of the University of Palermo, to examine the bones and file a report, which would be released to the public. Correnti accepted the job, with the understanding that he could not devote his attention full-time to the bones; he had teaching obligations at the university, and he was a much-sought-after guest lecturer at universities across Europe. With the approval of the pope, Msgr. Principi agreed to Dr. Correnti's terms.

Correnti understood that he would not be dealing with a complete skeleton, so he laid out all the bones in the three boxes on two tables, one for large bones, the other for small, making a checklist of what bones were present. He found that the sternum, or breast bone; the left tibia, or shin; and the left patella, or kneecap, were almost completely intact. There were also five biggish pieces of the ilium, or pelvic bone. Then he ran into a problem: there were three fibulas, the slender leg bone that runs parallel to the tibia. Where had the extra fibula come from, and whose was it?

Evaluation of the bones got even more complicated. Correnti

found pieces of four more tibias. It was obvious to the anthropologist that he was looking at bones from several individuals. In addition, he found about fifty pieces of bone that came from livestock—sheep, goats, horses, and cows. The remaining two hundred bones were human, but of how many humans Correnti could not yet say. To determine the gender, body type, and age at time of death would require precise, painstaking measurements of each bone and fragment.

Professor Correnti's work dragged on for years. Ultimately he concluded that the bones were from three individuals, two men and one woman. The men had both died in their fifties, the woman when she was about seventy. One of the men was of average build, the other more muscular. Correnti found that among the bones that came from the man of medium build, there were pieces of the skull and five teeth.

To nonspecialists, the presence of animal bones in a human grave may seem odd, but it did not surprise Correnti. At the time of Peter's death there were some farms in the neighborhood of the arena and the cemetery; some of the bones might have been dumped here after meals or washed here during heavy rainstorms, or in the case of the horses, buried after the animals died. They could have become mixed together when the grave was dug. The animal bones were not the problem; it was the human bones that were troubling, or more precisely, disappointing.

The archaeological team had been so hopeful that the bones Father Kirschbaum unearthed were those of St. Peter, but they were not experts in human anatomy. The medical team's examination of the bones had confirmed the archaeologists' optimism, but the physicians were not anthropologists. Professor Correnti delivered the unhappy news to Msgr. Principi in person. Based on his findings, he said, none of the bones from the grave belonged to St. Peter.

It was a crushing outcome, but not everyone at the Vatican was willing to accept Correnti's assessment. They clung to a phrase in the professor's written report that the bones from the seventy-year-old person were "almost certainly" female. It was more than just the term "almost" that buoyed their spirits, because in the case of the seventy-year-old there was no skull, not even fragments of skull bones. This fact dovetailed neatly with the skull said to be St. Peter's enshrined in the Lateran Basilica. As for Correnti, he filed his written report and stayed out of the debate that was churning around his conclusions.

· · • · ·

But Professor Correnti's work at the Vatican was not over yet. There were a few more boxes of bones found near the grave of St. Peter, and Professor Correnti agreed to examine these, too.

If the first three boxes of bones had proven to be a disappointment, Kirschbaum and his colleagues could console themselves that at least they had found the memorial, what the Roman priest Gaius had called the tropaion, of St. Peter. As they examined the structure more closely, they discovered that, typical of most construction projects, the second-century workmen had run into some unexpected problems. While digging a drainage ditch to protect the tropaion from water damage, they uncovered several humble pagan graves. If they followed the existing architectural plan, a portion of the memorial, the famous Red Wall (more on that shortly) would have covered most if not all of one of the graves, thereby depriving family and friends access to the resting place of their deceased loved one. This the builders would not do, so they altered the size of the tomb of St. Peter by half. In this restricted space Peter's skeleton could not lie at full length: the leg bones would have to be adjusted to fit within the smaller space. "Behavior of this kind might at first scandalize the modern mind and seem in contradiction with the great reverence that was paid to the apostle's grave," Kirschbaum writes. "We must be careful, however, not to project modern ideas and sentiments, conditioned by a devotion to St. Peter that has grown through the centuries, into an age that had not yet experienced that devotion." The archaeologist's point is that the builders of the tropaion did not regard moving St. Peter's bones as an irreverent act, but as an unavoidable necessity.

Kirschbaum also reveals another problem the movement of Peter's bones presented to the Church in Rome: Roman law demanded that if human remains were to be moved, a license must be obtained from the state, and an animal must be sacrificed at the grave to appease the offended spirit of the dead. Christians would not offer a pagan sacrifice—their cemeteries were filled with the bodies of men, women, and even children who had refused to participate in any pagan rite. So, in the case of St. Peter's tomb, the Christians almost certainly ignored the law and proceeded as if they had a license and had made the sacrifice the law demanded.

Chapter 5

MONSIGNOR KAAS'S BOX OF BONES

Monsignor Kaas had been an able administrator. No one faulted his supervision of the maintenance of St. Peter's. But he was not an archaeologist, and he understood very little about archaeological methods. Nonetheless, as the overseer of the physical plant of St. Peter's, he was nominally the head of the team excavating beneath the high altar. His greatest concerns were irreverence to holy ground and unnecessary damage to ancient structures. The four archaeologists shared Kaas's sensitivity, but looking at these objectives from the point of view of a professional archaeologist sometimes put them at odds with a man whose task it was to safeguard one of the most sacred sites in the Christian world. The tension created by these differing points of view was occasionally exacerbated when Kaas offered unsolicited, uninformed opinions about some facet of the dig. As a result, the resentments between the four archaeologists and Msgr. Kaas reached the point that they barely spoke to one another, meeting only when absolutely necessary to discuss some essential aspect of the excavation.

Kaas rarely went down into the necropolis to observe the digging, but each evening he and the foreman of the sampietrini, Giovanni Segoni, visited the site to observe the work of the day. Msgr. Kaas was especially concerned about any human bones that may have been found. The necropolis was a cemetery, and he believed that the remains of the dead should remain undisturbed, as their families had originally intended. He feared that by chance, when soil from the dig was hauled out of the excavation for disposal elsewhere, human remains might get mixed in. To prevent what he regarded as sacrilege, during his evening tours of the site Kaas would collect any bones he saw, placing them in lead-lined wooden boxes, and sending them to a storage facility for reburial in the necropolis at a later date.

In 1942, the evening of the day the archaeologists had found the blue-white wall covered with Christian graffiti, Kaas and Segoni came to inspect the site. Segoni saw the fissure at the bottom of the wall and shined his flashlight inside. He told Msgr. Kaas that there were bones within a marble chest set in a niche carved roughly into one wall. Kaas instructed the foreman to reach inside and remove the bones. Segoni also brought out some old coins, a piece of textile, and some metallic threads. The two men placed the debris, along with the bones, inside a box that Segoni labeled OSSA-URNA-GRAF, or "bones-urn-graffiti [wall]"; Msgr. Kaas then carried the box to a storage room in the Grottoes. He never mentioned to the archaeologists what he had found, nor what he had done with the bones.

A day or two later, when the sampietrini had opened up a

large opening in the graffiti wall and pushed Father Kirschbaum inside, no one had the least idea that Msgr. Kaas and Segoni had been there ahead of them and had removed human remains from St. Peter's tomb.

Msgr. Kaas kept the box of bones in storage until the end of his life in 1952. He never had them examined by any scientist of any kind. So far as is known, he never showed them to anyone. The nondescript box was just there, no more calling attention to itself than any of the other items in that storage room. When Msgr. Kaas died, Pope Pius had him buried in the Grottoes of St. Peter, among the popes, a token of the Holy Father's appreciation for his old friend's love for and dedication to the basilica.

• • • •

After Pius's announcement of the discovery beneath St. Peter's of a Roman necropolis that included the tomb of the first pope, the Vatican was besieged with requests to visit the excavation. Scientists of all kinds, journalists from almost every nation, not to mention pilgrims and the curious, wrote for permission. Most of these requests were denied. The excavations were in a fragile state, and nothing had been done as yet to prepare the site for visitors. Among the handful of experts who were given access to the necropolis was Professor Margherita Guarducci of the University of Rome (the school was also known affectionately as "La Sapienza"—"wisdom"). Guarducci was a scholar who specialized in epigraphy, or the study of ancient inscriptions. Arguably her most important fieldwork had been done on the island of Crete, where she had deciphered countless inscriptions in Greek and Latin. She had made significant contributions to deciphering the Gortyn Code, about six hundred lines of often-fragmentary text chiseled into a stone wall about 450 BC in Gortyn, an ancient city in southern Crete. Between 1935 and 1950 she published three massive volumes on the inscriptions she had studied in Crete and a fourth volume dedicated entirely to the Gortyn Code. Although her work mystified most non-specialists, among her peers Prof. Guarducci was one of the most respected archaeologists and epigraphers in the world.

Guarducci's work in the Vatican Necropolis began in 1952. She was less interested in the tombs and the Roman decorative art in the necropolis than in the inscriptions and the graffiti. She was escorted through the necropolis by Monsignor Francesco Vacchini, whom Pope Pius had named temporary administrator of St. Peter's immediately following Msgr. Kaas's death.

After a preliminary examination of the inscriptions, Prof. Guarducci characterized them as the "third voice" that testified to the authenticity of St. Peter's tomb beneath the basilica's high altar (the other two "voices" were the ancient authors, such as the priest Gaius, and the evidence found during the excavations of the 1940s). Guarducci estimated that the blue-white wall—known to archaeologists as Wall G—had been built ca. 250, then covered by Constantine's builders when they erected the original Basilica of St. Peter. The graffiti, therefore, dated from the period between ca. 250 and ca. 315. When the excavators uncovered it in 1942 they were the first human beings to see the wall in more than sixteen hundred years.

As with Father Kirschbaum, Guarducci was well aware of the tradition among the ancient Christians of leaving names and inscriptions on walls near the tombs of martyr-saints. In her book *The Tomb of St. Peter*, Guarducci cites examples such as the inscriptions found outside the crypt of the early popes in the Catacomb of St. Callixtus and near the tomb of the early-fourth-century martyrs Saints Peter and Marcellinus in the cemetery on the Via Casilina. "All these writings belong to the faithful," Guarducci writes, "who, close to the martyrs' remains, wished to leave a memorial of themselves or, more often, of their deceased friends and relatives."

The first wall Guarducci inspected in the necropolis was Wall G. It was this wall that had disappointed Kirschbaum and his colleagues because it did not bear the name of Peter. But Prof. Guarducci found the name of Peter inscribed at least twenty times. Generously, she excused her colleagues: "The first excavators of the Vatican necropolis, not recognizing the cryptographic system on this wall, could read and understand only a very small part of its inscriptions." In fact, Guarducci was the first scholar to examine Wall G closely. To her delight she found the wall's inscriptions to be "a wonderful page of Christian spirituality in which the names of Christ, Mary and Peter are particularly prominent and their victory is acclaimed."

The team of archaeologists who had not been trained in ancient Christian epigraphy as intensively as Prof. Guarducci did not know how to interpret what to them appeared to be incomprehensible scratches in the plaster. Guarducci revealed that those symbols were monograms, abbreviations, for the name Peter. She added that these same monograms have been found on everything from jewelry to tombstones to coins to household objects that date from the fourth and fifth centuries. "With the discovery of the symbol's meaning, we now have an idea of the immense popularity enjoyed by Peter during the early centuries of the Church," she writes.

Peter's name appears on Wall G in another interesting manner. Guarducci found the letters AP, APE, and APET, all abbreviations for the Latin phrase *ad Petrum* ("near Peter") almost always linked to the name of a deceased relative or friend. She says that the formula is found scratched into walls near the tombs of other Roman martyrs, such as St. Crescentianus and St. Hippolytus. Christians believed that by burying their beloved dead near the remains of a saint, the saint would intercede for the soul of the deceased, hastening his or her transit to heaven. The phrase is not only an expression of hope; it is also an assurance that the soul of a loved one is now near the saint, looking upon the face of God.

On Wall G, Guarducci found that the symbol for Peter was often inscribed beside the Chi-Rho monogram for Christ. In Matthew 16:17–19, Jesus gives Peter spiritual authority over the Church, so it would be a natural thing for Christians to link Peter's name with that of his Divine Master. (In later centuries, one of the pope's titles would be "Vicar of Christ.") Likewise, the letter M or the MA monogram for Mary also appears with the Chi-Rho, uniting Mother and Son just as the Peter symbol and the Chi-Rho unite the Master and his Apostle. The inscriptions on Wall G revealed that the early Christians appreciated both the spiritual and the natural affinity that existed among Jesus, Mary, and Peter.

But Guarducci found more. Wall G provided numerous examples of what Guarducci called a "cryptographic system," a code, in which the early Christians used letters of the Greek and Roman alphabets, along with arcane symbols, to convey some of the truths of their Christian faith. Of course, only the initiated would be able to interpret this code—a practice the Christians adopted from the pagan mystery cults that were flourishing at this time in Rome and elsewhere in the Roman Empire. According to Guarducci, both Christians and members of the mystery cults shared a predilection for the esoteric. Some of these signs have survived to our own day, such as the Greek letter tau (T), which now as then represents the cross. Other examples include the Chi-Rho monogram for Christ, and the alpha (A) and omega (O), the first and last letters of the Greek alphabet, which Christ had used to describe himself in Revelation 22:13. Guarducci observed that sometimes, in an inscription referring to a deceased Christian, alpha/omega was written OA, symbolizing "from the end to the beginning," meaning the passage from death—the end of mortal life on earth—to the beginning of eternal life in heaven. Another common emblem was an M superimposed on an A, an abbreviation for the Latin name Maria or Mary. This monogram found in the catacombs and other Christian cemeteries can be seen to this day in many Catholic churches, depicted in stained glass, embroidered on vestments, or carved into altars dedicated to the Blessed Virgin.

There were two other inscriptions Guarducci discovered that took the archaeological community by surprise. Above one of the many Chi-Rho monograms inscribed on the wall, and near the name of Leonia, a deceased Christian woman, Guarducci found the Latin phrase HOV or HOC VIN[CE], meaning "with this or by this, conquer." The inscription was a clear reference to an event in the life of Constantine. On October 27, 312, the eve of the Battle of the Milvian Bridge, in which Constantine would triumph over his rival and become emperor of Rome, he had a vision. Bishop Eusebius of Caesarea, the emperor's confidant and first biographer, describes the event in his *Life of Constantine*:

> *And while he was thus praying with fervent entreaty, a most marvelous sign appeared to him from heaven, the account of which it might have been hard to believe had it been related by any other person. But since the victorious emperor himself long afterwards declared it to the writer of this history, when he was honored with his acquaintance and society, and confirmed his statement by an oath, who could hesitate to accredit the relation, especially since the testimony of after-time has established its truth? He said that about noon, when the day was already beginning to decline, he saw with his own eyes the trophy of a cross of light in the heavens, above the sun, and bearing the inscription* CONQUER BY THIS. *At this sight he himself was struck with amazement, and his whole army also, which followed him on this expedition, and witnessed the miracle.*

Supernatural events tend be difficult, if not impossible, to authenticate. Some historians have suggested that either the story of the cross of light was invented by Eusebius to suggest that Constantine ruled with the blessing of Almighty God, or some anonymous copyist had interpolated the story into Eusebius's original text. The presence of the HOV or HOC VIN[CE] inscription on Wall G (in fact, there are two such inscriptions) indicates that the story was current among Christians of Rome soon after the Battle of the Milvian Bridge.

The inscriptions on Wall G proved to be an exciting find, particularly after Prof. Guarducci deciphered them. Once she completed her work on Wall G, she turned to the much older Red Wall.

Chapter 6

PAINFUL FACTS

The tangle of inscriptions scratched into the blue-white plaster of Wall G was an exciting discovery. The invocations of Jesus Christ, the Blessed Virgin Mary, and St. Peter; the expressions of confidence in eternal life; and the references to the vision of Constantine all combined to open a window into the spirituality of the early Christians of Rome. As significant as Wall G is to understanding Christianity in Rome during the first centuries of the life of the Church, the Red Wall would prove to be even more crucial in terms of the archaeological excavation beneath St. Peter's.

Based on the factory stamp found on the bricks of the Red Wall, Prof. Guarducci knew that the wall had been erected about 160. She estimated Wall G to have been built about 250. While Wall G was a confused mesh of graffiti, only one inscription was scratched into the red plaster of the Red Wall: two Greek words, PETR and ENI. Immediately after the I in ENI, the plaster had fallen away. Father Kirschbaum and his colleagues, who first spotted the inscription, believed that ENI was the first part of the Greek for "Peter in peace." This confession of faith in the eternal peace St. Peter enjoyed in the Kingdom of Heaven was perfectly in keeping with other early Christian inscriptions found at the tombs of saints and martyrs. Nonetheless, Guarducci believed that the archaeological team had misread the inscription.

Guarducci contended that the inscription PETR ENI was complete, and if that were the case, then the inscription would read in English "Peter is within." That was an exciting assertion, because it resolved any doubt as to whether this tomb directly below St. Peter's high altar was the grave of the first pope, the Prince of the Apostles. To defend her claim, Guarducci drew upon her expertise in ancient inscriptions. Citing "the vocabulary of tomb inscriptions," Guarducci explained that the verb ENI was often used to indicate that a dead body lay inside, or within, a tomb. Guarducci's explanation eliminated any possibility that the inscription should be read figuratively, that the "spirit" or the "memory" of Peter is recalled at this spot. According to Guarducci, the phrase PETR ENI should be taken literally—the body of St. Peter is inside this tomb.

Dating the inscription was a bit trickier. Almost all the inscriptions on Wall G had been in Latin, an indication that they were made in the third century at the earliest, a time when Greek was no longer fashionable as the common language of Rome and the people had returned to their native Latin. She argued that the Red Wall inscription was probably earlier, very likely around the time of the wall's construction, ca. 160, because,

Guarducci wrote later, "It is well known that the earliest Christian inscriptions in Rome are written in Greek, the common language of the first followers of the new religion." In 160, Greek was still widely spoken, read, and written by most Romans.

There is yet another difference between the Red Wall inscription and the Wall G inscriptions: the Wall G inscriptions were inscribed by pilgrims, but Guarducci believed PETR ENI was "a true and proper sepulchral epigraph . . . a sort of notation written to mark the exact location of the tomb." In other words, PETR ENI is comparable to a name carved into a headstone to identify whose body occupies the grave. It may have been scratched into the red plaster by the caretaker of the tomb or even by Pope St. Anicetus (r. ca. 157–168), who ordered the construction of the tropaion. In other words, "Peter is within" is not a casual graffito; it is an intentional inscription.

As if any more proof were required, another wall behind the Red Wall reinforced Guarducci's assertion, and that of the earlier archaeological team, that St. Peter's tomb had been a destination for pilgrims. This brick wall is covered with random drawings, what we would call doodles, as well as Christian inscriptions. A Greek inscription reads: EMNESTHE L. PAKKIOS EUTYCHOS GLYKONOS, or "Lucius Paccius Eutychus remembers Glycon." Guarducci explained that "so-and-so remembers so-and-so" inscriptions have been found all around the Roman world, typically at some significant place such as a shrine or landmark. If the spot had religious significance, both pagans and Christians (at their own respective sacred sites) would leave behind this inscription to show that they had remembered and prayed for a loved one at the shrine.

Guarducci argued that Lucius Paccius Eutychus must have been a Christian, because in the Vatican Necropolis there was nothing of significance to attract a pagan—no shrine to a god, no grave of a famous hero. The only notable buried in this cemetery was St. Peter, and only Christians would be drawn to his tomb.

Among the doodles on the wall Guarducci saw a drawing of a fish. As early as the first century, Christians used the fish as an emblem of their faith. They made the Greek word for fish, *ichthys,* into an acrostic: "Iesous Christos Theou Yios Soter," or "Jesus Christ, Son of God, Savior." As is the case with the best symbols, the fish had multiple meanings among Christians. Christ had called his apostles "fishers of men," an especially apt phrase since at least four of the twelve (including St. Peter) were fishermen. Converts were born into a new life by being drawn out of the water at baptism, just as fishermen drew fish from the sea. This metaphor was reinforced by the second-century theologian Tertullian, who wrote in his treatise *Concerning Baptism,* "But we little fish, like our Fish Jesus Christ, are born in water."

To summarize Guarducci's findings as briefly as we are doing here is misleading. It took five years of intense, concentrated labor before she arrived at her conclusions. Once she received Pope Pius's permission to study Wall G and the Red Wall, almost immediately Prof. Guarducci developed a routine. She spent her mornings in the Vatican Necropolis, examining the inscriptions in person. Then she spent her afternoons in the comfort of her office poring over photographs of the inscriptions. One morning in 1953—the year Pope Pius XII placed her in charge of all archaeological excavations at St. Peter's and the Vatican

(Guarducci was the first woman to hold the post)—she descended into the necropolis, where she found Giovanni Segoni, the foreman of the sampietrini, at work. They made small talk standing beside Wall G. The opening the workmen had made in 1943, through which Father Kirschbaum had entered the tomb, was still there. Casually, Guarducci asked Segoni if anything substantial had been found inside the tomb. Segoni said, yes, there were human bones. Guarducci asked if he meant the bones Father Kirschbaum had uncovered. No, he replied, this was a different set of bones. He explained his nocturnal visits to the necropolis with Msgr. Kaas, and the monsignor's anxiety regarding human remains uncovered in the course of excavation. Then Segoni told Prof. Guarducci a part of the story she had never heard before, that probably no one had heard before: at the order of Msgr. Kaas, Segoni had reached inside St. Peter's tomb and removed bones that lay inside a plain marble chest. He had placed the bones inside a wooden box, written a label identifying where they were from, and when he and Msgr. Kaas left the dig for the night, he had followed the monsignor to the storage room in the Grottoes, where the box of bones was placed among other items Kaas had taken from the necropolis. He knew exactly where the box was, Segoni said, and if the professor was interested, he could show them to her. Guarducci said that she was interested, so she followed him out of the necropolis up to a small, dark room.

Pilgrims to St. Peter's see only the splendor of the upper basilica and the papal tombs and tiny devotional chapels in the Grottoes. But behind the splendid facade is a warren of little rooms that serve a host of utilitarian purposes. The room to which Segoni led Prof. Guarducci held boxes of human bones from the necropolis, collected by Segoni at the direction of Msgr. Kaas to safeguard them from possible desecration. The monsignor had intended to have the bones reverently reburied in the necropolis, but he had died before he could fulfill his intention.

Segoni poked around among the boxes that were piled in no particular order until he found what he was looking for. He unlocked it and raised the lid. Inside, atop a pile of bones, lay a small paper label that read OSSA-URNA-GRAF. Prof. Guarducci laid the label aside, then removed each bone, one by one, and placed them on the table. There were long arm and leg bones, nearly intact, as well as vertebrae and smaller bones she could not identify. She also found a raggedy bit of purple cloth in which she discerned a few gold threads, and two coins, one dating from the Middle Ages, the other worn smooth and so unidentifiable. Guarducci had no expertise in human anatomy, so these bones meant nothing to her, except that they had been found inside St. Peter's tomb. The presence of the medieval coin suggested to her that these were the remains of some anonymous soul from the Middle Ages, perhaps a venerable priest or bishop who was granted the privilege of being buried near the relics of St. Peter.

She replaced the bones in the box, along with the label, the rag, and the coins. Segoni secured the lock; then Guarducci wrapped the box in heavy brown paper. At the time she did not attach any importance to this particular collection of bones—there was nothing distinctive about them—but as she explained later in her book *The Tomb of St. Peter*, "the elementary duty of serious scientific inquiry led me to transfer them to a dry place and to the making of provisions for their systematic examination by a qualified specialist." She carried the box to the main office of St. Peter's, where she explained to Msgr. Vacchini what she had found and suggested that at some future date the bones should be examined by experts. Vacchini agreed and had the box locked away in a cupboard.

· · • · ·

It took Prof. Guarducci five years to decipher the graffiti on Wall G and the Red Wall. By the time she completed her analysis in 1958, there was no doubt in her mind or that of the original archaeological team that they had indeed found the tomb of St. Peter. It was a severe disappointment, however, that the bones Father Kirschbaum found in the tomb were clearly not those of the apostle. Meanwhile, the box of bones Segoni had removed from St. Peter's tomb remained locked in the cupboard of the basilica's main office, all but forgotten.

In October 1962 Dr. Correnti completed his report on the Kirschbaum bones. In the interest of being as comprehensive as possible, he decided to analyze another collection of bones that had been found in the tomb by Segoni and Msgr. Kaas, and that Segoni had given to Guarducci nine years earlier. The box, still wrapped in brown paper as Prof. Guarducci had left it, was delivered to Correnti's lab. He peeled back the paper, unlocked the box, and began lifting out the bones. Unlike the Kirschbaum bones, these were the bones of a single individual. There were a few animal bones, but far fewer than in the Kirschbaum cache. There was also the complete skeleton of a field mouse, which Correnti guessed had squirmed into the locked box at some point and, unable to find its way out, died inside.

Once all the bones had been spread out on the lab table, Correnti found that he had the right and left thighbones; the right and left shins; and the right fibula, or lower leg bone. Correnti identified eight pieces of arm bones. The bones of both hands were almost complete. There were twenty-two pieces of the cranium, or skull; two pieces of the mandible, or jaw; and a single tooth. From the sutures on the cranium, Correnti could tell that the individual had been sixty or seventy years old at the time of death. But the bones of the feet, from the ankles down, were missing entirely.

After months of measurement and analysis, Dr. Correnti concluded that this individual had a robust build, stood about five feet seven inches tall, and was male. He had found soil clinging to some of the bones, an indication that originally the body had been laid in the bare earth in an ordinary grave without a coffin or sarcophagus. Some of the bones bore dark reddish stains. Given the presence of the purple fabric, Correnti put forward the hypothesis that at some point, after the decomposition of the flesh, this man's bones had been wrapped in purple cloth woven with gold threads. The purple dye had leeched into some of the bones, staining them dark red.

By the time Dr. Correnti had completed his study of the Segoni/Kaas box of bones in 1963, Pope Pius XII had been dead five years, and his successor, Pope John XXIII, was in the last weeks of his life. It was early June when Prof. Guarducci stopped by Dr. Correnti's lab. Just days earlier, Pope John had died, and the cardinals of the Roman Catholic Church were on their way to Rome for the papal funeral, followed by the conclave to elect a new pope. As two scientists working together at St. Peter's,

Guarducci and Correnti had become friends. That day in 1963 they discussed the box of bones, wondering who this man may have been. He must have been an important individual to be granted the distinction of burial inside St. Peter's tomb.

Although their conversation had been casual, for the next several days Guarducci could not get Correnti's findings out of her head. She approached Correnti again, and this time he suggested some scientific analysis of objects found with the bones, including the soil, the piece of fabric, and the chips of marble. But Guarducci would need authorization from the pope for these tests, and at that precise moment there was no pope.

·· • ··

On June 21, 1963, Cardinal Giovanni Battista Montini was elected pope. He took the name Paul VI. By chance, Cardinal Montini was a longtime friend of the Guarducci family. Prof. Guarducci requested a private audience with Paul, but as a new pope his calendar was overcrowded with appointments with leading churchmen, Vatican bureaucrats, foreign diplomats, and heads of state. His secretary informed Prof. Guarducci that the pope's schedule did not have an opening until November 1963. Guarducci accepted the November appointment and waited.

On the appointed day, Prof. Guarducci arrived with copies of her newly published book on the tomb of St. Peter, which she presented to the Holy Father. Then she delivered her news: she was all but certain that the actual bones of St. Peter had been found. Dr. Correnti had completed his rigorous examination of the bones; now, to confirm his findings, Guarducci asked the pope's permission to conduct several more tests. Intrigued,

Paul gave his consent and expressed the wish that Dr. Correnti should make the additional tests at once.

Guarducci's news was tantalizing. Dr. Correnti's analysis of the bones removed from the tomb by Father Kirschbaum had been a bitter disappointment to the late pope Pius XII and members of the Vatican household, who had hoped that the relics of St. Peter would be found in the necropolis. Since the Kirschbaum bones were without a doubt not St. Peter's, and since no other bones had been found in the tomb (or so everyone believed), there was one question on everyone's mind: What had become of the relics of St. Peter? Now Prof. Guarducci and Dr. Correnti were saying that there was a strong probability that a second set of bones taken from the tomb—and virtually forgotten for a decade—were the true remains of the Prince of the Apostles.

On that day in November, Pope Paul had no more time to give his old friend. He was planning to spend Christmas in the Holy Land, and preparations for the pilgrimage were occupying most of his working day. He promised to meet with Guarducci in the New Year.

The pope kept his word. In January and again in February he met with Guarducci and Correnti. At one of their meetings, the two scientists brought along the box that held what they believed to be the bones of St. Peter. With the pope's authorization, they were proceeding with the tests of the soil, of the piece of textile found with the bones, and of the animal bones mixed among the human bones. Now the scientists had one more request, one much more sensitive than the other three: they wished to open the Lateran Basilica reliquary said to contain the skull of St. Peter. Portions of the cranium and a piece of the jawbone had been found in the loculus, the marble chest; Guarducci and Correnti wanted to compare the bones from the necropolis with the bones enshrined in the reliquary.

This was a delicate issue. The Catholic Church throughout the world possesses many relics, some of which have a better provenance than others. During the Middle Ages, the desire to possess a truly remarkable relic led some churches and abbeys and even private collectors to display objects that are perhaps best described as dubious. One church, for example, claimed to own the shield of St. Michael the Archangel; another asserted that it had a feather from the Holy Spirit. By the 1960s, most of these implausible relics had been removed from the public view and packed away as curious antiques.

There was no documentary record of the translation of the skulls of St. Peter and St. Paul from their tombs to the Lateran Basilica. Oral tradition asserted that the skulls had been venerated for many years in the Sancta Sanctorum, the pope's private chapel in the Lateran Palace across the street from the church, but there was no surviving document to confirm that. There was a document from the eleventh century that stated the skulls were enshrined above the high altar of the Lateran Basilica, but that was the earliest surviving record.

Inside the Lateran Basilica, a Gothic marble canopy stands over the high altar; it soars two stories high, taller than any other medieval canopy in Rome. The upper portion is a large relic chamber. Behind a bronze grill one can see the two reliquaries said to contain the skulls of St. Peter and St. Paul. In 1799, when Napoleon occupied Rome, he sent a detachment of his troops to the Lateran to confiscate the reliquaries. During the French Revolution, violent mobs often ransacked churches, broke the shrines of the saints, and burned the bones. Napoleon's troops were better disciplined: they only wanted the reliquaries, so they simply left the skulls behind. When the relics were brought to Pope Pius VII, he was relieved to find that the seal of Pope Urban V, the last pope to examine the relics personally, was intact and unbroken on the wrappings.

By permitting Guarducci and Correnti to examine the contents of the reliquary of St. Peter, Pope Paul was running the risk of discovering that the relic at St. John Lateran was fraudulent. Ultimately, Paul decided to take the risk, but he set some conditions. The scientific analyses of the contents of the Segoni/Kaas box would be supervised by the administrator of St. Peter's, Monsignor Primo Principi, and conducted at the laboratories of the University of Rome. In the case of the examination of the bones from the Lateran reliquary, however, Pope Paul insisted that the analysis must be conducted in the privacy of the Vatican workrooms.

Among the human bones in the Segoni/Kaas box were the bones of livestock—horses, cows, goats, the types of animal remains one would expect to find in a rural area. The hypothesis that the mouse found a way into the box but couldn't find a way out was confirmed, too. The tiny skeleton was complete, which would have been highly unlikely if Segoni had grabbed it up with the other, larger bones. Furthermore, the mouse's bones were clean and no soil clung to them, a sure sign that the little creature had died inside the box rather than in St. Peter's tomb.

Also found inside the Segoni/Kaas box of bones were bits of

marble; Guarducci had these fragments tested, and the results revealed that they were from the same marble slabs that lined the loculus in St. Peter's tomb.

An oral tradition told how the Saracen raiders broke open St. Peter's shrine and scattered his bones. Guarducci called in whom she described as "the best specialists in Roman wall-construction." After examining the loculus, they concluded that from the day Constantine began construction of his basilica around 325, until the day in 1943 when Father Kirschbaum squeezed his head and shoulders inside the tomb, the loculus had never been tampered with. The story of Saracen sacrilege had no basis in fact.

Next, Guarducci called for analysis of the soil that clung to some of the bones. It was found to be a mix of yellow sand and blue clay—a perfect match with the soil inside the tomb.

The tests of the bit of purple fabric produced a surprise. The cloth was ordinary wool, but the gold threads were special. Using powerful microscopes, the scientists found that the gold threads had been produced in two ways. Some were made up of a thin coat of gold applied over a woolen thread, a painstaking process, but simple compared with the second method of making gold threads. The second method took a linen thread, wrapped a layer of copper acetate around the thread, and then a layer of gold. This complicated technique was developed late in the era of the Roman Empire, about the third century. "The gold was genuine," Guarducci reported. "The cloth was dyed with purple made from murex." Murex is a large sea snail that yields a purple dye, used in ancient Rome and elsewhere to color royal robes and sacred vestments. Finally, examination of the pattern of the weave concluded that it was typical of Rome.

Once all the test results had been collected and examined, Prof. Guarducci felt sufficiently confident to advance a theory. Sometime after the Edict of Milan put an end to the persecution of the Church in Rome, someone, perhaps representatives of the pope or representatives of the emperor, or perhaps a group made up of Christian clergy and government officials, entered the tomb, exhumed Peter's remains from the grave, wrapped them in purple cloth, and laid them inside the marble chest in the loculus, which had probably been made for this purpose. Guarducci believed the transfer of the bones had been done for both religious and practical reasons. As the first pope and a much-venerated martyr, St. Peter deserved a better burial than lying in bare earth. And, Guarducci observed, "probably the well-founded fear that the dampness of the earth, which is notoriously very considerable in the Vatican area, would rapidly damage the venerable remains which had once been entrusted to it."

Segoni had found the bones inside this marble box. Unlike the bones Father Kirschbaum dug out from a crevice beneath the tomb, the bones from the loculus belonged to a single individual, a robust man who was between sixty and seventy years old at the time of his death. "From this concise exposition," Guarducci wrote, "it can be seen that the above elements constitute the links of a chain, joined to one another, and that chain leads to a conclusion: the bones of Peter have been identified."

· · ● · ·

The identification of the bones from the Lateran reliquary was not so straightforward. When the reliquary arrived at the Vatican workroom and was opened by Correnti and his colleagues, they found that it did not contain a complete human skull, but several small fragments of cranium, a small piece of the jawbone, and several vertebrae. The cranial bones were too small for the scientists to determine either gender or the individual's age. Nonetheless, they spent several months studying the bones, making meticulous notes, photographing every relic and every step of their process. Paul VI wanted a complete scientific report, but he had added a caveat: no matter what conclusion was reached by Correnti and his colleagues, the pope would decide if, when, and how the report would be made public.

After several months of study, Correnti and his team came to two conclusions. First, there were not enough physical remains to say anything definitive about the individual whose bones were enshrined in the Lateran reliquary. Second, there was nothing about these bones that ruled out the possibility that at some unknown date they had been taken from St. Peter's tomb to be venerated elsewhere.

Correnti and his colleagues were using the best analytical tools available in the mid-1960s. Today, twenty-first-century medical science would use DNA tests to see if any of the bones in the Lateran reliquary match the bones from the loculus of St. Peter's tomb.

Correnti filed his report on the Lateran relics in 1964. The analysis of the contents of the Segoni/Kaas box and of the Lateran bones was complete—eleven years after Giovanni Segoni first showed the box of bones to Prof. Guarducci. With all the scientific data assembled, Guarducci got in touch with the four-man team that had led the excavation of the Vatican Necropolis: Professor Enrico Josi; Father Antonio Ferrua, S.J.; Father Engelbert Kirschbaum, S.J.; and Bruno Maria Apollonj Ghetti.

Her story of Msgr. Kaas's custom of removing bones from tombs and mausoleums took them all by surprise. Her revelation that Giovanni Segoni, at Msgr. Kaas's orders, had removed bones from the loculus in St. Peter's tomb and kept them in a storeroom in the Grottoes left them incredulous. When Guarducci revealed the test results of the loculus bones and the bones Father Kirschbaum had uncovered, Josi, Ferrua, and Apollonj Ghetti refused to believe the report.

For more than two decades they had believed that the bones Father Kirschbaum passed out of the tomb had been the remains of St. Peter. True, at the time they had not subjected the remains to any type of scientific analysis, but they had always been convinced that the discovery of the bones from the tomb of St. Peter marked the pinnacle of their professional careers. They had restored to the Church an inestimable treasure—the true relics of St. Peter. Now Prof. Guarducci was telling them that the bones they had found had no religious significance at all, and that the bones that in all probability were the remains of the first pope had been found by their nemesis, Msgr. Kaas. It was hard news to hear, and of the four, initially only Father Kirschbaum could bring himself to accept the facts, however painful and disconcerting.

Chapter 7

ARCHAEOLOGY ISN'T ALGEBRA

In 1964, Prof. Guarducci published *The Tomb of St. Peter,* her account of the discovery of the tomb and relics of St. Peter. To this day, it makes for disappointing reading. In a misguided attempt to protect the feelings of the original archaeological team, who were still deeply disappointed that the bones they had found in Peter's tomb were not the relics of the apostle, and unwilling to sully the memory of Msgr. Kaas, Guarducci did not tell the full story of the exploration of the tomb, or of Giovanni Segoni and Msgr. Kaas's private evening visits to the excavation and their removal of the bones from the loculus in St. Peter's tomb. Consequently, Guarducci's book has a once-over-lightly feel to it that reads more like a work of wishful thinking than a scientific report of an important archaeological find.

She left out so much information that her account of the excavation sounded vague. What she cited as evidence was thin. And her conclusions appeared unsupported by scientific data.

As a result, when she asserted that the true bones of St. Peter had been found, a host of critics rejected her claim, arguing that the evidence she cited was insufficient to make such a remarkable assertion. The more generous critics said that the best that could be said of the bones was they were possibly the remains of St. Peter. Author John Evangelist Walsh, who chronicled this unhappy period in Prof. Guarducci's career, wrote, "A misguided wish to shield the reputations of all concerned had clouded [Guarducci's] usual good sense, leading her to try the impossible—gaining acceptance for the relics while telling less than the full truth." This was a serious misstep that inadvertently played into the hands of critics, who even rejected the idea that Peter had ever been in Rome.

· · • ·

For almost thirteen hundred years, no Christian disputed that St. Peter the Apostle had traveled to Rome, where he established the Church and subsequently was martyred and buried. Catholics, schismatics, and heretics of all stripes were at least united on this point. Even during the most bitter years of strife between the Holy Roman Emperors and the popes, when denial that Peter had founded the Church in Rome might have undermined the authority of the pontiff and strengthened the emperor's assertion that by right he should be the foremost power player in Christendom, no emperor asserted that the tradition of Peter in Rome was a self-serving myth fabricated by the papacy and its supporters.

In the twelfth century, the tradition was challenged by the Waldensians, a tiny, proto-Protestant sect whose members lived in a remote valley of the French Alps. No one took the Waldensian denial seriously, not least because they were notorious for refusing to accept any religious text except the Bible.

Then, in 1324, Marsilius of Padua, rector of the University of Paris—at the time the most distinguished school of theology in western Europe—wrote a book titled *Defensor Pacis* (*The defender of peace*)—in which he denied that St. Peter was ever in Rome. "But, as to Peter," Marsilius wrote, "I say that it cannot be proved by Scripture that he was bishop of Rome or, what is more, that he was ever at Rome. For it seems most amazing if, according to some popular saint's legend, St. Peter came to Rome before St. Paul, preached there the word of God and was then taken prisoner, if then St. Paul after his arrival in Rome acting together with St. Peter had so many conflicts with Simon Magus and in defense of the faith fought against emperors and their agents, and if finally, according to the same story, both were beheaded at the same time for their confession of Christ, there fell asleep in the Lord, and thus consecrated the Roman Church of Christ—most amazing, I say, that St. Luke, who wrote the Acts of the Apostles and Paul himself make not the slightest mention of St. Peter."

In spite of Marsilius's impressive academic credentials, his rejection of the Peter-in-Rome tradition did not attract broad attention until the nineteenth century, when the issue became the target not of historians, but of religious polemicists. In 1862, Thomas Collins Simon published *The Mission and Martyrdom of St. Peter: Or, Did St. Peter Ever Leave the East?* Historian of the Peter tradition Daniel William O'Connor describes Simon as a zealot who believed that it was "incumbent upon a Protestant to attack every stand taken by the Roman Catholic Church concerning the primacy of Peter, lest by some small concession or admission the position of Protestantism be compromised."

Perhaps because at this time the issue was always couched in fiercely partisan terms, the debate concerning Peter in Rome was not taken up in the universities. This is doubly strange given that many universities in the late nineteenth century had begun to use the historical critical method to examine both Sacred Scripture and sacred traditions. It was not until the early twentieth century that the Petrine tradition was examined critically by professional historians. Protestants such as Paul Wilhelm Schmiedel, a theologian and professor of the New Testament at the University of Zurich, and Charles Guignebert, a professor of the history of Christianity at the Sorbonne in Paris, rejected the Peter-in-Rome tradition. So did some Catholic scholars, including Louis Marie Duchesne, a historian of Christianity who was also a Catholic priest. Ironically, Ernest Renan, an expert on the history of early Christianity who was admired by Schmiedel, Guignebert, Duchesne, accepted the Peter tradition. Writing of the early Christians, Renan said that the infant Church in Rome was "reinforced by the coming of Peter, who became its head."

Catholic scholars responded to the critics by pointing to texts from the New Testament and the early Fathers of the Church. In the Gospel of John, Jesus says to Peter, "When you were young you girded yourself and walked where you would; but when you are old, you will stretch out your hands, and another will gird you and carry you where you do not wish to go. (This he said to show by what death he was to glorify God)"

(John 21:18–19). To stretch out one's hands was a euphemism in the Roman world for crucifixion, the death that tradition claims Peter suffered. John's gospel is thought to have been written sometime between the years 85 and 100, twenty years or more after Peter's martyrdom, so that would make the evangelist a reliable source of how Peter died (although the gospel does not say where).

As for the historicity of Peter's residing in Rome, St. Peter himself gives readers a hint in his first epistle. At the conclusion of his letter, he says that he is writing from a particular Christian community, "She who is at Babylon" (1 Peter 5:13). "Babylon" among the first Christians was an allegory, or code, for Rome. Babylon/Rome is also referred to several times in Revelation. Defenders of the traditional view cite these New Testament texts as proof that Peter did live and die in Rome.

There are a few more early sources supporting the Peter-in-Rome tradition. In his letter to the Christians of Rome, St. Ignatius of Antioch, writing ca. 110, said, "I do not give you orders like Peter and Paul." The statement suggests that Peter and Paul governed the Church in Rome. The statement also tells us that the Peter-in-Rome tradition was accepted as fact both by Christians outside the city (Ignatius came from Antioch) as well as Roman Christians.

About the year 200, the North African Christian philosopher and apologist Tertullian wrote in his *The Prescription Against Heretics*, "You have Rome, from which there comes even into our own hands the very authority of apostles themselves. How happy is its church, on which apostles poured forth all their doctrine along with their blood! Where Peter endures a passion like his Lord's! Where Paul wins his crown in a death like John's [St. John the Baptist]." This is rather late, but it adds another interesting bit to the puzzle: by 200, the story of Peter's death by crucifixion and Paul's by beheading was accepted across the Roman world.

Finally, there is a source we have mentioned before, Gaius's letter, written in 199, to the heretic Proclus, offering to take him to see the graves of St. Peter and St. Paul outside Rome.

To religious believers as well as some professional historians, these texts are convincing documentation that St. Peter resided in Rome and was martyred and buried there. Other historians will urge a more cautious approach. Writing in his foreword to *Peter in Rome*, Frederick C. Grant, president of Seabury-Western Theological Seminary in Evanston, Illinois, stated that biblical and postbiblical literary evidence for the Peter-in-Rome tradition amounted to "hints, innuendoes, shy and obscure references."

· · • · ·

Professor Guarducci's book on the tomb of St. Peter was not the first time one of her works had come under fire. In 1958 she published *The Graffiti Under the Confessio of St. Peter in the Vatican*, a three-volume account of her analysis of the inscriptions on Wall G. Her most ferocious critic was none other than Father Antonio Ferrua. Writing of Guarducci's deciphering of the inscriptions, Ferrua said, "Thus one can either commiserate with or admire the illustrious Authoress for her immense exertions, carried out with commendable passion and ingenuousness, and indeed with a faith that ought to move mountains.

But all this cannot suffice to make us accept a work that is fundamentally wrong."

Prof. Guarducci and Father Ferrua had had a difference of opinion before: in the early 1950s they diverged on the reading of the Christian inscription inside the Valerii mausoleum in the Vatican Necropolis. Father Ferrua had looked at it closely, of course, and he concluded that the inscription was too faded, too indistinct to decipher. Daniel William O'Connor, author of *Peter in Rome: The Literary, Liturgical, and Archaeological Evidence,* tells us that Guarducci studied the inscription for one solid year (1952–1953). Within the first five months, she believed she had cracked the code. In November 1952, Guarducci presented her initial findings to members of the Pontifical Roman Academy of Archaeology. She revealed that the inscription read:

PETRVS ROGA XS HIS	*Peter, pray to Christ Jesus*
PRO SANC(TI)S	*For the holy*
HOM(INI)BVS	*Christian men*
CHRESTIANIS AD	*Buried near your body*
CO(R)PVS TVVM SEP (VLTIS)	

For Guarducci, this was incontrovertible evidence that the body of St. Peter lay nearby. But dating the inscription would be as tricky as deciphering it. Guarducci had found what she believed was an important clue: inside the Valerii mausoleum she saw a sculpture that she believed represented Emperor Marcus Aurelius, whose reign began in 161. That sculpture set the earliest possible date for the inscription. The latest date at which it could have been scratched into the wall was ca. 325, when Constantine began construction of the Basilica of St. Peter. That was a very broad spectrum of time, but there was no other evidence in the graffito or the tomb to enable Guarducci to date this invocation of St. Peter more precisely.

On one point, however, Prof. Guarducci and Father Ferrua concurred: both read the inscription on the Red Wall as PETR ENI, "Peter is within." That reading made Ferrua the target of critics, some of whom argued that the Jesuit was indulging in wishful thinking, that the incomplete inscription actually read "PETR END[EI]," or "Peter is not here." It was a provocative reading that demanded more than scholarly speculation. Why would a Christian write such a thing on the tomb wall? Had Peter's body been within the tomb at one time, but then moved elsewhere? In that case, the inscription could be seen as the ancient equivalent of a forwarding address.

There was a longstanding tradition that in 258, during a period of fierce persecution under the emperor Valerian, Christians had moved the remains of St. Peter and St. Paul from their tombs to a new burial place in the Catacomb of St. Sebastian, outside Rome on the Appian Way. On the walls near the reputed hiding place of the relics are countless graffiti invoking St. Peter and St. Paul. According to this tradition, at some point after the death of Valerian in 260, the relics were returned to their original tombs.

Most of the critics of Guarducci's book were less sneering than nitpicking. Some focused obsessively upon the bit of purple cloth that had been found among the bones in the loculus. The cloth appeared to be deep red in color—was this the result of fading over the centuries or a chemical reaction to the soil, bones, and perhaps the marble of the loculus? What was the actual shade of "purple" in imperial Rome? Some scholars argued it was reddish, or violet, or even mauve. And just because a reddish rag had been found with the bones did not mean that the dead man was St. Peter. Perhaps he was an anonymous distinguished Roman, or a man who in life had wanted to be taken for a distinguished man and so he wore clothing that suggested purple. Such second-guessing tormented Guarducci for months after the publication of her book.

She tried to respond. In the case of the cloth, she took some threads to a colleague, a chemist at the University of Rome. To bring back the original color of the cloth, the chemist applied a drop of hydrosulfite to the thread—it suddenly became bright red. Was that shade of red what the Romans meant when they spoke of "purple"? No one was certain.

Another objection was the marble loculus. Skeptics dismissed Guarducci's claim that the box had been undisturbed for sixteen hundred years. Guarducci recruited experts in ancient Roman construction methods and escorted them down to St. Peter's tomb. With Pope Paul's permission, they dismantled the marble chest, taking out each slab and examining it closely. They also examined the brick walls of the loculus. All the experts agreed that the brickwork was undoubtedly ancient Roman. There was no sign of damage to the bricks or to the mortar. There were no chisel marks, no broken bricks or bricks of a later period, no trace of crumbled mortar that was replaced by mortar that had been mixed according to a different formula. Everything was intact and uniform, as pristine as the day the marble slabs had been set in place. In other words, there was no evidence that the loculus had ever been damaged or disturbed.

Other critics wanted to know why Correnti had not had the bones from the marble chest radiocarbon-dated. Correnti replied that radiocarbon dating would have required the destruction of a large bone; as it was within the realm of possibility that these bones were the relics of St. Peter, neither the scientists nor Pope Paul VI were willing to authorize such a course of action. Furthermore, radiocarbon dating in the 1950s and 1960s was not precise; it could only give an estimated age, within a plus or minus factor of one hundred years.

Yet other critics objected to identifying the bones as those of St. Peter when they may have been the bones of an anonymous early martyr or pope or much-venerated churchman. To answer this objection, Guarducci summarized all the existing evidence: the unbroken sixteen-hundred-year-old tradition that St. Peter's tomb lay beneath the high altar of St. Peter's Basilica; the discovery of the tomb itself by the Vatican archaeological team; the inscriptions invoking Peter on the blue-white wall; the "Peter is within" inscription on the Red Wall; the care Constantine had taken to enclose the tomb in a white marble shrine and position the high altar of his basilica over St. Peter's tomb. Finally, while many Christians and early popes had been buried near St. Peter's tomb, it was unlikely that any would have been granted the privilege of being buried inside the tomb with the Prince of the Apostles. All of this evidence led the scientists who had been studying the necropolis, the tomb, and its contents since the early 1940s to conclude that the bones found in the loculus were most likely the bones of St. Peter. There simply was no evidence that those bones belonged to anyone else.

Even the removal of the bones from the grave to the marble box became a target for carping. Some put forward the idea that it was irreligious of whoever it had been who disturbed St. Peter's remains to put them in a marble box. Others alleged that the marble box was too simple a receptacle, that something much grander and more lavish would have been appropriate for the bones of the first pope. Critics who argued that it was sacrilege to move the remains of a saint from a grave to a shrine overlooked a practice known as translation; it was just beginning in the Catholic Church in the fourth century and it is still practiced today. The translation is the formal removal of relics from the grave or the original tomb to a shrine, typically within a church or chapel. Now that Christians were at liberty to build churches, the practice of moving relics into a church picked up momentum. In the eighth century, when the catacombs were in a sad state of neglect and entering them was becoming dangerous, the pope authorized the translation of the remains of countless martyrs into the churches of Rome, and even sent relics to churches in other lands. Today, opening the grave of a candidate for sainthood and moving the remains to a shrine is part of the Catholic Church's canonization process.

In 1967, Prof. Guarducci answered her critics in a pamphlet. It was not enough to quell the firestorm of criticism and second-guessing directed at her book, but after the publication of the pamphlet, she wrote no other defense of her work. On the subject of the tomb and relics of St. Peter, Margherita Guarducci was done with public debate.

Within the Vatican, any doubts or debate on the subject were settled by Pope Paul VI. On June 26, 1968—twenty-eight years after the excavations beneath St. Peter's had begun—the Holy Father made a startling announcement during his weekly general audience. The bones of St. Peter had been found. "New analyses—very patient and very detailed—have been made," Paul said, "which led to results which, relying upon the opinion of competent and careful experts, we think positive: the relics of Saint Peter have been identified in a way which we consider as persuasive." The pope continued: "It is our duty to announce to you and to the Church this happy news."

The next day, a small procession descended into the Grottoes of St. Peter's Basilica, then down to the necropolis. Pope Paul, wearing upon his head a miter, one of the emblems of a bishop, with a red cope draped over his shoulders (red is the liturgical color for martyr saints), led about a dozen churchmen to St. Peter's tomb. Two members of the laity were in the procession, as well—Dr. Venerando Correnti and Prof. Margherita Guarducci. In keeping with Vatican protocol, Prof. Guarducci wore a black dress and a black lace veil.

A table had been set beside the tomb, and arranged upon it were nineteen sturdy, custom-made clear Plexiglas boxes. Inside each box were the bones of St. Peter, arranged by body part: skull bones in one, vertebrae in another, and so on. Attached to each box was a label identifying the type of bone and declaring that these were the relics of St. Peter. One box contained the bones of livestock that had been found with St. Peter's relics, and another box held the skeleton of the mouse.

As the pope and his attendants looked on, Prof. Guarducci

and Msgr. Principi handed the boxes, one by one, to Dr. Corrrenti, who arranged them inside the marble chest in the loculus, where Giovanni Segoni and Msgr. Ludwig Kaas had first seen the bones one evening twenty-six years earlier. After all the boxes were in place, sampietrini sealed a glass panel over the opening of the tomb. Pope Paul offered a prayer. Then a Vatican notary read an official account of the proceedings, which would be filed in the Vatican Archives. One of the workmen swung shut and locked a heavy bronze gate. Through the grill, everyone could see the Plexiglas boxes lying inside the marble box. Then Pope Paul led the small congregation out of the necropolis and back to the magnificent basilica above them.

While many Catholics rejoiced at the announcement that the relics of St. Peter had been found, the response among their Protestant friends, as well as members of the scholarly community, was more reserved. The editors of *The Christian Century*, a leading American Protestant journal, wrote: "We cannot get too excited about the to-do in Rome occasioned by Pope Paul's announcement that 'the relics of St. Peter have been identified in a way that we believe convincing.' . . . But assuming that the bones are of the man Catholics consider the Prince of the Apostles and the first bishop of Rome, we, unlike Pope Paul, do not feel bound . . . to honor sacred relics. Indeed, we make no bones about the fact that we are perverse enough—Protestant enough—to believe that no bones, not even a saint's, are sacred."

In February 1969, Graydon F. Snyder, dean and professor of New Testament studies at Bethany Theological Seminary and at the Chicago Theological Seminary, published in the journal *The Biblical Archaeologist* an assessment of Paul's announcement and of the conclusions contained in the reports on the excavation of the Vatican Necropolis. "For whatever reasons the Pope made the statement," Snyder wrote, "be it the appropriateness of the 19th centennial [of Peter's martyrdom] or sheer political sagacity—the effect will be to suffocate one of the most intriguing questions in archaeology." In other words, Paul VI had effectively shut down any further discussion or debate on whether St. Peter's remains had survived to the present day.

The account of Msgr. Ludwig Kaas's removal of the bones from the loculus in the tomb and of Giovanni Segoni's revelation to Prof. Guarducci years later stretched Snyder's credulity. He couldn't imagine that Kaas would act in such a high-handed, secretive manner that the team of archaeologists would not have known that he had tampered with the tomb, that no one would have found the bones in the decade that followed. Summing up this story, Snyder wrote, "It becomes difficult for me to distinguish between fact and fiction, truth and gossip, debate and slander." He was perhaps overlooking the possibility that resentments and petty jealousies can exist even among scholars.

In the end, Snyder adopted the position of the editors of *The Christian Century*: "Probably in the long run the bones of Peter will not be so important a matter. What will be of lasting value is the fascinating picture we have gained of church life in the early centuries." This was a thoroughly professional assessment. By the late 1960s, archaeology downplayed any notion that members of their field were treasure hunters like Howard Carter, the English archaeologist who discovered the tomb of the boy-pharaoh Tutankhamun. Modern archaeologists did not look for fabulous artifacts; they sought to understand the day-to-day lives of people who lived in a particular place at a particular time. Certainly the Vatican Necropolis provided a vivid snapshot of Roman burial customs, both pagan and Christian, in the first centuries of the Christian era. Yet, however much *The Christian Century* editors and Prof. Snyder would like to dismiss it, the excavation had also yielded a treasure—the bones of St. Peter. For Catholics, Orthodox, and other Christians, that was a big deal. It was not a big deal for all Catholics, however—*America* magazine, the leading Jesuit newsweekly in the United States, never reported Pope Paul's announcement.

A year later, Daniel William O'Connor published his *Peter in Rome,* in which he concluded: "No certain statement can be made concerning Peter's Roman residence, martyrdom, and burial." He argued that the testimonies of the author of the Gospel of John, St. Ignatius of Antioch, and Gaius are all late, that there is no testimony earlier than the final decade of the first century. Nonetheless, O'Connor was evenhanded in his criticism— he pointed out that there is also no documentary evidence from the first century or the centuries afterward that states that Peter was never in Rome, or that perhaps he came for a time and then left.

In O'Connor's mind, when studying the Peter-in-Rome tradition, one enters the realm of "possibilities and probabilities." Gaius had no doubt that the tropaion on Vatican Hill sheltered the bones of St. Peter. Tertullian in far-off Carthage had no doubt that Peter and Paul had served the first Christians of Rome and had died with them. The anonymous Christian pilgrims who scratched their petitions into the plaster of Wall G and the Christian member of the Valerii family who inscribed a prayer to St. Peter inside his family tomb also had no doubt that they were near the burial place of Peter. If the early Christians believed Peter had lived and died in Rome and was buried there, why did so many contemporary archaeologists and scholars deny it?

As O'Connor wound down his arguments, he was careful to be exact. In terms of the location of St. Peter's tomb, he says, "We must speak in terms of belief, not in terms of true or false. We must ask where was it believed that Peter was buried and how early is the evidence which we find for that belief?" Ultimately, O'Connor rendered a decision that would please some, but not all: he concluded that it was probable that Peter resided in Rome, that he was martyred there, and that the Church in Rome honored his memory. As for the recovery, burial, and later enshrinement of Peter's body, O'Connor was skeptical. As a condemned criminal, the Roman authorities would have had Peter's corpse taken from the cross and tossed into the Tiber. O'Connor believes that marking the site of a "grave" and identifying the "bones of Peter" were inventions of devout Christians years later and done "for apologetic reasons"—primarily the assertion of the spiritual supremacy of the bishop of Rome over the entire Catholic Church.

That is one point of view. Writing in 2004 in *Letters to a Young Catholic*, George Weigel, the distinguished Catholic author and biographer of Pope John Paul II, said, "Archaeology isn't algebra; it yields probabilities rather than certainties. But reputable scientific opinion today holds that the excavations under St. Peter's in the 1940s—originally undertaken for an entirely different purpose—did yield the mortal remains of Peter."

Weigel's statement "Archaeology isn't algebra" gets to the heart of this question. In a society that (by and large) places its trust in science, people have become accustomed to certainty. But in the case of St. Peter's bones, certainty is impossible to establish. The DNA of Peter the fisherman vanished almost two thousand years ago, so there is nothing to compare against the DNA of the bones Giovanni Segoni removed from the marble box inside Peter's tomb. Margherita Guarducci believed absolutely that the bones were the bones of St. Peter. Pope Paul VI concluded that such faith was reasonable. Others have disagreed and will continue to do so, but their objections have not persuaded a vast multitude of believers.

EPILOGUE

Father Engelbert Kirschbaum, S.J., did not live long after Pope Paul VI's announcement that the bones of St. Peter had been found. In March 1970, he died in Rome and was buried in the city's German Cemetery, the Campo Santo Teutonico, the only cemetery inside Vatican City.

Margherita Guarducci returned to teaching, holding classes at the University of Rome (La Sapienza) and Rome's National School of Archaeology, where she served as director until 1978. In 1980 she became involved in controversy once again when she published a book that stated that the golden Praeneste fibula (also known as the brooch of Palestrina) was a forgery. The brooch had been discovered in 1887 by archaeologist Wolfgang Helbig, and it was considered a treasure as its inscription—dated to the seventh century BC—was the earliest example of the Latin language. Guarducci argued that the brooch was a hoax that had been fabricated by Helbig and an art dealer and forger named Francesco Martinetti. The question was settled in 2011 when two scientists, Edilberto Formigli and Daniela Ferro, conducted chemical analysis of the brooch and found that it was genuine. Margherita Guarducci did not live to see her conclusions regarding the fibula overturned; she died in Rome in 1999 at the age of ninety-seven.

Father Antonio Ferrua, S.J., never accepted that the bones from the loculus were those of St. Peter. Until 1984 he served as director of the Sacred Museum of the Vatican Library. Father Ferrua's list of publications was itself a library: during his lengthy career as a scholar he published approximately 420 books and articles. His most impressive work was a multivolume translation of more than forty thousand Christian inscriptions in Rome. In 2001, Pope John Paul II marked the occasion of Father Ferrua's one hundredth birthday by sending him a papal blessing as well as his thanks for his many years of distinguished service to the Holy See. Father Ferrua died in 2003 at the age of 102.

Bruno Maria Apollonj Ghetti continued to work for the Holy See. From 1972 to 1975 he directed the cleaning and restoration of the Church of Santa Maria della Pietà in Camposanto dei Teutonici, a fifteenth-century church inside Vatican City. Apollonj Ghetti also served on the faculty of the University of Bari. He died in Rome in 1989 at the age of eighty-three.

In 1966, Dr. Venerando Correnti moved from the University of Palermo to the University of Rome. From 1991 to 1993 he was director of the university's Institute of Anthropology. He died in Rome in 1991 at age eighty-one.

The Second Vatican Council, which had been called by Pope John XXIII, concluded its work in 1965 under Pope Paul VI. The aftermath of the council would haunt Paul's pontificate and color his reputation after his death. Paul tried to introduce reforms that modernized and streamlined Catholic life while preserving Catholic doctrine and the authority of the papacy. It was a difficult balancing act, and, sadly, Pope Paul was not especially good at it. Liberals among the clergy, religious, and laity viewed the council as a complete rupture with the past. Invoking "the spirit of Vatican II" rather than what was written in the conciliar documents, they implemented an agenda that was virtually unthinkable a decade earlier. Catholic colleges and universities shed their distinctively Catholic identity. Bishops ignored instructions from Rome; priests and nuns refused to obey their superiors; laypeople defied their pastors. Priests and nuns abandoned their religious vocation by the tens of thousands. Dissent from Catholic teaching erupted around the world and was exacerbated when, in 1967, Pope Paul published an encyclical enforcing the rule of clerical celibacy and then, in 1968, an encyclical upholding the Catholic Church's ban on artificial methods of birth control. In spite of the papal encyclical, millions of Catholic married couples, particularly in the United States and Western Europe, decided on their own that they could use birth control and still be good Catholics.

The most dramatic departure of all came in 1969, when Paul introduced the Novus Ordo Missae, the new way of saying Mass. It was such a dramatic departure from the way Mass had been said for centuries that traditional Catholics came to believe that perhaps the Vatican Council had repudiated "the old Church," while liberals concluded that in terms of liturgical life, "anything goes." The tide was against traditional and even moderate Catholics, and Paul was unable to stop it. He died on August 6, 1978, largely unappreciated by any of the various factions within the Catholic Church. He asked to be buried in the Grottoes of St. Peter's, in a simple tomb with no monument.

Today the Scavi ("the Excavations"), as the Vatican Necropolis has come to be called, is open to visitors, but not many. Groups are limited to 15, children younger than twelve are not admitted, and tickets must be reserved months in advance. As a result of these restrictions, it is a rare day that more than 250 fortunate individuals see one of the most remarkable sites in Rome. Compare that minuscule number to the thousands who throng the Basilica of St. Peter and the Vatican Museums nearby. But the restrictions are necessary for two reasons. First, the tombs, the graves, the carvings, the frescoes, and all the other artifacts are fragile; large crowds moving among these ancient structures would inevitably do some damage, but small groups of mature adolescents and adults are easier to control. Second, at the heart of the Scavi is a shrine—the tomb of St. Peter, with his relics displayed within. This is holy ground, and once again, crowds of tourists or even well-intentioned religious pilgrims would undermine the solemnity of this place.

To visit the Scavi is to leave twenty-first-century Rome behind and step into first-century Rome. The atmosphere is damp—nothing can be done about that; to preserve the frescoes from fading, the lighting is subdued. The tour takes about ninety minutes, led by a guide who is extremely well informed about the Scavi. The tour concludes at the tomb of St. Peter. George Weigel, writing of his visit to the Scavi, said, "What we've just seen and touched and smelled is about as close to the apostolic roots of the Catholic Church as it's possible to get."

Appendix A

LIST OF SYMBOLS

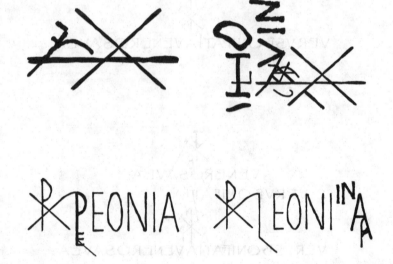

VENEROSAVEA
VERVBONIFATIA

VERVSBONIFATIAVENEROSAVEA

VENEROSAVEA
VERVBONIFATIA

VERVSBONIFATIAVENEROSAVEA

VENEROSAVEA
VERVBONIFATIA

VERVSBONIFATIAVENEROSAVEA

Appendix B

WHAT ABOUT ST. PAUL'S BONES?

During the night of July 15–16, 1823, a fire broke out in the timber roof of Rome's Basilica of St. Paul Outside the Walls. Workmen repairing the roof had been careless with the brazier of hot coals used to melt the lead. Unobserved, several coals had fallen out of the brazier onto the roof. At some point after dark, the smoldering coals burst into flame.

The fire first swept through the ancient timbers, bringing the roof crashing down. The cave-in crushed venerable altars and shrines, pulverized sculpture, and leveled row upon row of columns, many of which the original builders had taken from ancient Roman structures. In some parts of the basilica, the fire burned so hot that marble was completely consumed and reduced to piles of lime. By morning, the fifteen-hundred-year-old basilica, Rome's last surviving basilica built by Constantine, lay in ashes.

Inspection of the ruined church revealed some good news:

the transept had survived, as had the marble Gothic canopy carved by Arnolfo di Cambio in 1285 and installed over the high altar. The tomb of St. Paul the Apostle, which lay beneath the high altar and Cambio's canopy, had escaped the fire unscathed. Nonetheless, Cardinal Ercole Consalvi, the pope's secretary of state, could not bring himself to tell the sad news to Pius VII, who was confined to his bed, seriously ill. The pope's doctors feared that he was dying. Pius had endured a long, often difficult, and for a time dangerous pontificate. The pope had often been at odds with Napoleon, and for a four-year period had been Napoleon's prisoner in France. Given Pius's frail condition, Consalvi feared that if he informed the pope that St. Paul's had been destroyed, the shock would kill him.

As news of the disaster spread across the globe, donations to rebuild the church poured in from Catholics and non-Catholics alike. The Russian Orthodox tsar, Nicholas I, sent slabs of priceless green malachite and lapis lazuli. The Muslim khedive of Egypt sent ten lovely alabaster columns. The response was so generous that by 1854, St. Paul's—rebuilt as a replica of the original basilica—was complete and ready for Pope Pius IX to reconsecrate it.

Unlike the tomb of St. Peter, the tomb of St. Paul had always been accessible to pilgrims. Before the high altar there was a *Confessio,* similar to the one at St. Peter's, with a balustrade and a flight of stairs leading down to a small chapel. Through a bronze grill one can see the tomb chest that bears the simple inscription PAUL APOSTOLO MART (Paul, Apostle and Martyr). Virgilio Vespignani, the architect of the reconstruction, wanted to open the apostle's sarcophagus, but the pope forbade it. The tomb and the remains of St. Paul were too sacred to be the object of scientific study, let alone curiosity.

According to an ancient tradition, St. Paul was beheaded during Nero's persecution of the Church. Paul was a Roman citizen, a distinction he inherited from his father. It was Rome's policy to grant citizenship to non-Romans as a way to build up a community loyal to Caesar in every province of the empire. Roman citizens enjoyed a number of privileges: they had the right to vote, to enter into legal contracts, and to contract a marriage recognized under Roman law. In addition, if a Roman citizen were charged with a crime, he could demand to be tried by Caesar. Furthermore, if a Roman citizen were found guilty of a capital crime, he was guaranteed a clean, painless death. As a result, Paul was spared the cruel, degrading death so many of his fellow Christians (including St. Peter) suffered at the hands of Nero.

It is said that St. Paul was beheaded at a spot occupied today by the Tre Fontane Abbey (Abbey of the Three Fountains). A chapel stands on the reputed site of his martyrdom. Displayed inside the chapel is the truncated column on which the apostle is supposed to have laid his neck and waited for the executioner's blow. There is a story that St. Paul's severed head bounced three times before it came to rest, and at each place where it struck the ground a spring bubbled up. These three springs can also be found inside the chapel.

After the execution, Christians carried Paul's body and head to a cemetery on the Via Ostiense, the road that leads to the port city of Ostia. Over this grave, Constantine erected the basilica subsequently known as St. Paul Outside the Walls.

To commemorate the two thousandth anniversary of the birth of Paul the Apostle, Pope Benedict XVI declared June 2008–2009 the Year of St. Paul and encouraged the Catholic faithful to mark the year with renewed devotion to St. Paul and careful study of his epistles. The holy year concluded on June 28, 2009, the eve of the Feast of St. Peter and St. Paul. Benedict traveled to the Basilica of St. Paul Outside the Walls for vespers, or evening prayer. In his homily, the pope made a dramatic announcement: he had permitted scientists to drill a tiny hole into the sarcophagus believed to hold the remains of St. Paul. Through this microscopic opening, the scientists inserted a camera-like probe. Inside they saw pieces of bone, blue linen cloth, and a purple linen robe adorned with gold leaf, as well as grains of red incense. With Benedict's permission, the investigators removed tiny bits of bone, which they sent to a laboratory for a carbon-14 test. To eliminate any possibility of a biased analysis, the scientists did not reveal the origin of the bones to their colleagues. "The fragments proved to belong to someone who had lived between the first and second centuries," Benedict announced to the congregation in the basilica and to the whole world. "This would seem to confirm the unanimous and undisputed tradition which claims that these are the mortal remains of the Apostle Paul. All this fills our hearts with profound emotion."

The pope's announcement did not go unchallenged. The next day Rengert Elberg, a Dutch archaeologist, anatomist, and expert in the study of ancient human and organic remains, told the German Press Agency, "It's impossible to establish that it's [St. Paul]." The fact that the bones came from a sarcophagus marked with Paul's name was intriguing, as was the dating of the bone fragments, but neither of these things was conclusive scientific evidence that the person inside the sarcophagus was St. Paul the Apostle. A DNA test would establish the identity, but there is no descendant of Paul to which the DNA results could be compared.

Nonetheless, Elberg suggested one way to make the identification somewhat more plausible. Tradition says that Paul was beheaded, and according to Elberg, "Traces of beheading can be identified with absolute certainty." He suggested moving the entire sarcophagus to a laboratory with a controlled environment, where the chest could be opened without damaging the fabric or the bones within. In such a setting, scientists could undertake a comprehensive examination of the remains. No such examination was authorized by Pope Benedict, and it is unlikely that his successor, Pope Francis, will permit it either.

BIBLIOGRAPHY

Aradi, Zsolt. *Pius XI: The Pope and the Man*. New York: Hanover
House, 1958.

"Bones of Contention." *Christian Century* 84, no. 28 (July 10,
1968): 888–89.

Brown, Peter. *The Cult of the Saints: Its Rise and Function in Latin
Christianity*. Chicago: University of Chicago Press, 1981.

Curran, John. "The Bones of St. Peter?" http://www.hissheep.org
/catholic/the_bones_of_peter.html.

Deutsche Presse-Agentur. "No proof that Vatican bones are
St. Paul's, says Dutch expert." http://news.monstersandcritics
.com/europe/news/article_1486637.php/No_proof_that
_Vatican_bones_are_St_Paul_s_says_Dutch_expert.

Emerson, Ephraim. *The Defensor Pacis of Marsiglio of Padua: A
Critical Study*. Cambridge, Mass.: Harvard University Press,
1920.

Eusebius. *The Life of the Blessed Emperor Constantine*. Nicene
and Post-Nicene Fathers, 2nd ser., vol.1, edited by Philip

Schaff and Henry Wace. Grand Rapids, Mich.: William B. Eerdmans, 1955.

Falasca, Stefania. "The Humble Splendor of the First Witnesses: The Catacombs of Saint Callixtus in Rome." *30 Days*, no. 4 (1996). http://www.ewtn.com/library/homelibr/callixt.txt

Guarducci, Margherita. *The Remains of St. Peter*. saintpetersbasilica .org/Docs/RemainsofPeter.htm

Guarducci, Margherita. *The Tomb of St. Peter: New Discoveries in the Sacred Grottoes of the Vatican*. Translated by Joseph McLellan. Hawthorn Books, 1964.

Hirschfeld, Amy K. (International Catacomb Society). "The Intellectual History of Catacomb Archaeology" (draft). http://divinity.uchicago.edu/martycenter/conferences /thedead/private/hirschfeld.pdf.

Ignatius of Antioch. "Epistle to the Romans." *Ante-Nicene Fathers*, vol. 1, edited by Alexander Roberts, James Donaldson, and A. Cleveland Coxe. Buffalo, NY: Christian Literature Publishing Co., 1885.

"Is it harmful to be upside down?" *BBC News Magazine*, September 24, 2008. http://news.bbc.co.uk/2/hi/uk_news /magazine/7633617.stm.

James, M. R., trans. *The Apocryphal New Testament*. Oxford: Clarendon Press, 1924.

Kirschbaum, Engelbert, S.J. *The Tombs of St. Peter & St. Paul*. Translated by John Murray, S.J. New York: St. Martin's Press, 1959.

Krautheimer, Richard. *Rome: Profile of a City, 312–1308*. Princeton, NJ: Princeton University Press, 1980.

Mueller, Tom. "Inside Job." *Atlantic Monthly*, October 2003, 138–42.

Murphy-O'Connor, Jerome. *The Holy Land: An Oxford Archaeological Guide from Earliest Times to 1700*. New York: Oxford University Press, 1998.

Northcote, Rev. J. Spencer, and Rev. W. R. Brownlow. *Roma Sotterranea or an Account of the Roman Catacombs Especially of the Cemetery of St. Callixtus*. London: Longmans, Green, and Co., 1879.

O'Connor, Daniel William. *Peter in Rome: The Literary, Liturgical and Archaeological Evidence*. New York: Columbia University Press, 1969.

Pastor, Ludwig. *History of the Popes*, vol. 6.

Ricciardi, Giovanni. "Peter's Martyrdom—A.D. 67 or 64?" *30 Days*, no. 3 (1996).

Biblical Archaeology Society. "Roman Crucifixion Methods Reveal the History of Crucifixion: Crucifixion in Antiquity." *Bible History Daily*, July 17, 2011. http://www.biblicalarchaeology.org/daily/biblical-topics/crucifixion/roman-crucifixion-methods-reveal-the-history-of-crucifixion/.

Scullard, H. H. *From the Gracchi to Nero: A History of Rome from 133 BC to AD 68*. 5th ed. London: Routledge, 1982.

Shanks, Hershel. "Scholars' Corner: New Analysis of the Crucified Man." *Biblical Archaeology Review*, November/December 1985, 20–21.

Snyder, Graydon F. "Survey and 'New' Thesis on the Bones of Peter." *Biblical Archaeologist* 32, no. 1 (February 1969): 2–24.

Early Christian Writings, Clement of Alexandria: Stromata (Miscellanies). http://www.earlychristianwritings.com/clement.html.

Tacitus, *Annals*.

Tertullian. *Against Praxeas VIII*. Translated by Peter Holmes. Ante-Nicene Fathers, vol. 3, edited by Alexander Roberts, James Donaldson, and A. Cleveland Coxe. Buffalo, NY: Christian Literature Publishing Co., 1885.

Toynbee, Jocelyn, and John Ward Perkins. *The Shrine of St. Peter and the Vatican Excavations*. London: Longmans, Green and Co., 1956.

Tzaferis, Vassilios. "Crucifixion—The Archaeological Evidence." *Biblical Archaeology Review* 11 (January/February 1985): 44–53.

The Holy See. http://www.vatican.va.

Walsh, John Evangelist. *The Bones of St. Peter: The First Full Account of the Search for the Apostle's Body*. Garden City, NY: Doubleday, 1982.

Weigel, George. *Letters to a Young Catholic*. New York: Basic Books, 2004.

Wiedemann, Thomas. *Emperors and Gladiators*. New York: Routledge, 1995.

Zander, Pietro. *The Vatican Necropolis*. Rome: Elio de Rosa, 1995.

Printed in the United States
by Baker & Taylor Publisher Services